BILOXI
RHAPSODY

"Giant Oak Trees Adorned With Spanish Moss"

"Geants chenes orne de mousse espagnole"

Biloxi Rhapsody

Memoires of a Storyteller

By

**Rhone` Sonnier Louviere`
(Ronnie James Sonnier)
and
Barbara Miller Sonnier**

Edited by: Barbara Miller Sonnier
and
Rhone' Sonnier Louviere'

Genre Tags: Drama-Education-Adventure-Travel-Poetry-
Inspiration-Literacy-Religion-Memoir-Faith-Young Adult-
Historical-Teen-Anthologies-Parenting-Christian-Self
Improvement-Family Relationships-Human Rights-
Symbolism-Assimilation-Patriotism-Biloxi, Mississippi-
Acadian Cajun French-Short Stories

ISBN-13: 9780615752990 (Rhone` Sonnier Louviere`
and Barbara Miller Sonnier)

FIRST EDITION
(Revised/Republished 1-2-2018)

Book design by Barbara and Ron Sonnier
Edited by Barbara Miller Sonnier and Ron Sonnier

Introduction

Biloxi Rhapsody: "Giant Oaks Trees Adorned With Spanish Moss"

By: Louviere`, Rhone` Sonnier, Born February 13, 1944

I am Rhone`, a 68 year old Caucasian American, a Cajun, code named Pop, and I have been writing my memoirs, about assimilation, faith, symbolism, and patriotism, in my head for most of my life. I, Rhone`, dared not write most of my life experiences down on paper for fear of ridicule until my experiences could be related with some semblance of credibility.

I, Rhone` Sonnier Louviere`, a US Army Vietnam Era Veteran, 1962-65, have visions, dreams, and or nightmares of incidents from long ago. Names have been withheld from military accounts in order to observe military decorum (code names have been used). There is no mal-intent in this, my memoir, towards the Vietnamese people, US Military or other entities.

One particular incident was a special black covert operation that occurred in Vietnam in July 1962, and it is this recurring nightmare and subsequent spiritual experience which propels me even deeper into my past to a point where I am obsessed with finding the facts about my military brothers, Snicker and Nickel.

The truth surrounding my own family and that of my soulmate and childhood sweetheart, Barbara Miller Sonnier's family (wife of fifty years) are written to describe cultural assimilation in Biloxi. I have experienced tragic incidences during my entire life. When a child of less than five years of age, I was confronted by a castaway dog named Gumbo and an alligator, and much later in my life in a harrowing experience where I, along with two of my men, are saved by a Phantom Spirit.

7

A mental plague of visions, dreams, and nightmares compel me to mentally exploit the past through conversations with my Daddy, wife Barbara, brother Joe, and research. This is a search to separate embellished fact from outright fiction. Memories of my mentors words and actions are always paramount in my mind, as I trudge on with life's new and challenging experiences. I realize that with each new incident I have the experience and acumen to handle it and move forward.

I, Rhone`, from a young age had fantasies of completing higher education. I have a Bachelor of Science Degree from The University of Southern Mississippi; a Master of Science from Abilene Christian University; and I have aspirations toward a Doctorate in Public Policy/Sociology from Duke University in Durham, North Carolina (I dream it and then I do it).

I roamed restlessly as I changed career paths, traveling state to state, and to countries throughout the world. I want to write it all down in a quest to try and make some sense of my worth in life, to my wife and my children, and to myself.

In my timorous visions and dreams, Biloxi, Mississippi is the back drop early on, and throughout my life, while an ominous warehouse occupied by French speaking fisher people, and farmers, in Vietnam, is at the epicenter of my most dreaded nightmare.

"Due preparations for the plague," by: Hospital, Jeanette Turner born 1942. "In this murky world of endless aliases and surveillance, who can be trusted? When does the quest for truth become a dangerous obsession? When does the assembling of facts tip into paranoia? And what difference can the truth make? Hospital probes with astonishing acuity the worlds of espionage and intelligence gathering, and the painful meaning of survival."

8

In Loving Memory

of

Bryan Keith Sonnier

"Giant Oak Tree Adorned With Spanish Moss"

"Biloxi Sojourner Spirit"

Biloxi is born,
opens his eyes,
looks to heaven,
sees the stars,
sun,
and moon.

Biloxi stands,
and turns,
sees the mountains,
rivers,
and forests,
and kneels before God.

Biloxi stands
and turns,
He and his blood spirits
sojourn the earth,
as man,
to do God's work.

By: Rhone` Sonnier Louviere`, November 28, 2012

9

Biloxi Rhapsody:
Memoirs of a Storyteller

A Memoir about Assimilation, Faith, Symbolism and
Patriotism
(Memoires d`une Teller Histoire)

Description of Words/Terms/Relatives

For the purpose of this book, I am Ronnie James Sonnier
(Rhone` James Sonnier Louviere`). My children call me
Daddy (known by many of my students simply as Pop).

Barbara Ann Miller Sonnier, my wife and soulmate, I call
Barbara, our children call her Mama.

Barbara's natural father is R. L. Miller and her mother
Sally Ann Goff (maiden name).

Carl Kemper Simmons, Barbara's father, the good man
who raised her from the age of two.

My brother is Mervin Joseph Sonnier, US Navy Petty
Officer Retired.

My middle name is James (Christian name) while Sonnier
is my father's last name and Louviere` is my mother's
maiden name.

Barbara and I have sisters and brothers, as well as, other
relatives who may be introduced and described in time,
within the body of each incident. Each individual is
introduced according to their own worthiness, and my
discretion in this my memoir.

Biloxi Indians:
In the Choctaw language they call themselves Taneks
haya, first people, and were believed to be of a small
Siouan tribe of South Mississippi.

Rhapsody:
A portion of an epic poem adapted for recitation; miscellaneous collection; highly emotional utterance; highly emotional literary work; effusively rapturous or extravagant discourse, rapture, ecstasy.

Synonyms: cloud nine, elatedness, elation, euphoria, exhilaration, heaven, high, intoxication, paradise, rapture, ecstasy, seventh heaven, swoon, transport.

Antonyms: depression.

Mate: A mate is more than just a friend, it is a term that implies a sense of shared experience, mutual respect and unconditional ... sister soul ... *(as âme is feminine in French) - compagnon - and un compain/une copine* to talk about buddies, or *mon copain* R. L. = R. L., one of my buddies ...

God's Song: The Holy Bible.

Foreword

As taken from King James Version of the Holy Bible

Book of Joel, Chapter 2, Verse 28, King James Bible (1611 Edition) *Your old men shall have dreams; your young men shall have visions:*

Book of Acts, Chapter 2, Verse 17, King James Bible (1611 Edition) *Your young men shall see visions, and your old men shall dream dreams:*

Book of Luke, Chapter 13, Verse 28, King James Bible (Cambridge Edition) *There shall be weeping and gnashing of teeth, when ye shall see Abraham, and Isaac, and Jacob, and all the prophets, in the kingdom of God, and you yourselves thrust out.*

Dedicated To

Barbara Miller Sonnier
Soulmate of mine / L`ame soeur de la mienne

and

Allen "Pete" Sonnier

and

Lois Hebert

and

Jo`El Sonnier

CONTENTS

Incidents

commencer (francais)
(Start)

Evangeline I

Evangeline and Gabriel were separated on their wedding day during the expulsion of the Acadians from *Acadie* (present day Nova Scotia, Canada). "Evangeline" is a sad and tragic fictional poem depicting their struggles to be together.

In 1847, Henry Wadsworth Longfellow wrote "Evangeline." Longfellow wrote of the travails of the French, many of whom suffered the same or similar plight as Evangeline and Gabriel's fictitious families. Many families were torn apart without mercy by kings claiming lands and powers at the expense of many cultures, not just the French settlers on Grand Prix.

Evangeline is beautiful poetry describing love lost and found again. Any culture or people would wish to claim a laudable part of the accounts as part of their own family history. None the less, the love of Evangeline and Gabriel as portrayed in "Evangeline" by Longfellow is fiction, not truth.

There are many historical facts in the poem, "Evangeline," that lend credibility to the migration of French settlers. However, "Evangeline" is a work of fiction. Any and all subsequent poems and stories by fine legitimate writers are also a mild form of plagiarism of Longfellow and the legend of Evangeline to aggrandize their own heritage and or that of their friends.

The precise plight and travails of the French poor and revolutionaries from France to Grand Prix and other islands is quite often a false rendering of historical accounts often resulting, in my opinion, in writer malpractice.

Acadian Cajuns

Cajun French individuals are smart and studious. Many Cajuns feel that they have lived and do live their lives as well-meaning people making contributions to society wherever they live in the shadow of the legend of Evangeline and Gabriel. Most Cajun French have never read or even heard of the poem "Evangeline" by Longfellow, but some Cajuns have heard stories and songs with Evangeline and Gabriel content.

Let us not give Longfellow too much credit. "Evangeline," the legend, existed long before he was born. Longfellow's poem only adequately depicts the legend of fictional characters in a sad tale portraying true love and injustice by The Crown upon helpless squatters and or sharecroppers. People without rights who were forced to migrate and settle elsewhere (destinations unknown), families torn apart and names changed forever. The Cajun French people's expulsion and subsequent migration started in France and spanned the earth.

The true account of Acadian Cajuns is more romantic and tragic than "Evangeline" or other well-meaning works portray. Cajuns have progressed to much more than the servants of others. Cajuns are a diverse people with an enlightened discerning spirit which emits kindness and compassion. Cajuns do not disdain and or otherwise avoid hierarchical relationships in working environments (this is an outright falsehood conjectured by false history prophets).

Cajuns are now an integral part of our American fabric, and most are gentle and of kind spirit. This truth is realistic and romantic enough without reminiscing about "Evangeline," the myth. Similar to the American Indians, such as the Biloxi or Choctaw, Cajuns are not wasteful. Condescension toward the mental capacity of Cajuns only unveils and exposes the ignorance of those who wish to elevate themselves by means of sinister nuance and deception.

In 1990, while I was completing my Masters' Degree in Education Supervision at Abilene Christian University, in Abilene, Texas, my wife Barbara and I were conversing with a new group of friends. Introductions were made and questions were posed regarding our last name and my nationality. I responded that I was French. After the introductions, we turned to walk away, and I overheard and witnessed one loving and kind young lady roll her eyes with comprehension as she said under her Christian breath, "Brothers and Sisters, he is a Cajun." The woman's statement was said in a belittling manner. I told Barbara what I had witnessed, and we were both disappointed and hurt.

I looked back at those Good Christians as Barbara and I left and never returned to that House of God again. The church we attended in Abilene was not and is not associated or affiliated with Abilene Christian University or McMurry University. The gesture and inference in a warm and peaceful church setting was particularly unsettling and hurtful. One does not expect this type of behavior from a Christian in a church building. Forgiveness is in my heart; I cannot forget injustice; I am not stupid. Cajun French are Americans. As I write these words my heart and the intellect of my soul are at peace, and I offer my hand in Cajun friendship (with a Red Rose) and brotherly love to all people.

My Louviere` family (Belgium) and Sonnier family (France) migrated to Grand Prix, Nova Scotia, Canada, New Brunswick; down and across these United States through Virginia (Shenandoah Valley), down the Ohio river, through Tennessee to Louisiana, Texas and Mississippi. My Papo (Sylvester Louviere`) and my Mamo (Laura Louviere`) left the sugarcane, corn, and rice fields, where they had been sharecroppers, and took their large family to Biloxi, Mississippi. The Louviere's

18

decided that they would explore life and work on the Mississippi Gulf Coast. After they arrived in Mississippi they worked in the seafood industry.

The entire migration of Acadian Cajuns is complex and interesting, therefore I intend to describe only the cultural history which I am most familiar with while testifying and witnessing to the assimilation journey of the Louviere` family of Mamo and Papo, and the family of Grandpa (Ursin) and Grandma (Olivia, nee Seymour) Sonnier of Mississippi and Louisiana respectively into mainstream American culture.

My people, Acadian Cajun French, are not Migrating Economic Parasites, whereas, we join in and contribute to the culture wherever we build our homes and or travel the world. We are Cajuns; some historical improvisation has inferred that we dislike or find disagreeable hierarchical influence. In fact we find dictatorship and taxation without representation reprehensible and will not stand for it being imposed on Cajuns or any other culture in America. We Cajuns are not revolutionaries; we are good neighbors and we are Americans. We understand that proper learning is the root of a successful free society.

My Mother, Annie Mae Louviere` Sonnier, is Caucasian French, and my Father, Dalton Joseph Sonnier, is Caucasian French. My Mother stood about five foot five inches tall, had a light olive complexion, and long wavy auburn hair. Mama, as we children called her, was slender with a long waistline, strong long slender legs, and very slight buttocks. In her youth, she worked in the sugarcane, corn and cotton fields in or near New Iberia, Louisiana.

The Louviere` and Sonnier families had been share-croppers. All the children toiled in the fields. My Mama finished the second grade, and my Daddy finished the fifth grade. Each joined the family in the fields when they were eight years of age. Both families had been

sharecroppers on oil land and later in life my Uncle Rene`
Sonnier and his eldest sister, my Aunt Mae Sonnier,
would legally prove this historic point. It would take over
twenty years of litigation, but finally a settlement for the
Sonnier sharecroppers paid off as a lucrative settlement
for each remaining sibling.

My Daddy, as his children call him, led the same or very
similar existence as my Mama. Daddy grew up near
Rayne, Louisiana. (Unfortunately, the Louviere` family
had no Rene` or Mae that worked on their behalf with the
oil company representatives. My Mother's family never
received a dime in recompense for their part ownership of
land.) The Sonnier and Louviere` families sharecropped
on land in and around Jennings, Louisiana.

All Cajun men hunted, fished and cooked. Some of the
women would accompany the men hunting and fishing,
and they were great at both. Rabbit, squirrel, quail, robin,
deer and wild pig were all game hunted and cooked for
meals. *Filet` Gumbo*, *Jambalya* and *Etouffee* (ay too fay)
with crawfish were some of the meals prepared.

My Mama and other relatives told me that my Daddy was
quite the cowboy. Daddy had his own horse. The horse
was a frisky black stallion which sported a beautiful black
saddle. Daddy wore black clothes, black boots adorned
with silver buckles, spurs, a white hat and a dark scarf
tied around his neck. Daddy worked long hard hours and
would save as much money as possible to use toward his
wardrobe and horse (he wanted to look as presentable as
possible when not in the fields with his six brothers, six
sisters, and his Father). Daddy, like other Cajuns, looked
forward to *Fais-do-do*.

I remember that my Dad was very handsome (and still is);
some people thought he resembled Dale Robertson, the
actor. When Daddy was younger he had an olive
complexion, light blue eyes, and wore his black curly hair
combed back in the Latin style. He was slender and stood

five foot eleven inches in height. *Giant Oak Tree Adorned With Spanish Moss.*

Daddy was dressed in his Fais-do-do attire, spurs and all, when he first met my Mama, Annie Mae Louviere`, at a dance hall in Louisiana (his horse was hitched to the outside rail). At the dance hall, as accordions and fiddles played along with a French horn and singing, the radio behind the bar played in the background (television had not arrived).

There was Cajun dancing, *Fais-do-do.* When it became late, Cajun children in attendance at a *Fais-do-do* were told to go to sleep, *Fais do-do.* Therefore, these dance parties became known as *Fais-do-do*, a Cajun dance. Cajun music was born from ballads, but has transformed to dance…*maison*, or a public dance in a dance hall called a *Fais-do-do*, this name for a Cajun dance party originated before World War II.

Cajun dancing with clapping and Cajun language dominated the talking on the floor as the bartender served drinks. The bartender (in his Cajun dialect) shouted for the band and dancing to stop as he turned the sound on the radio up higher and higher. The bartender said, "My God, the radio is saying that we are being invaded by Martians or some kind of aliens from outer space." The bartender continued shouting over the noise of the huge crowd of revelers, "We are being invaded somewhere up north or somewhere in a farmland."

On Sunday, October 30, 1938, millions of radio listeners were shocked when radio news alerts announced the arrival of Martians (aliens from outer space). The bartender said, "I am closing the saloon (dance hall), and I am going home right now." People panicked when they learned of the Martians ferocious and seemingly unstoppable attack on Earth. People ran out of their homes screaming while others packed belongings in their cars or horse drawn carriages and fled.

Annie Mae Louviere` (Mama) was single, twenty-two years of age, and she and her partner, Dalton (Nole) Sonnier (Daddy) who was nineteen, were on the dance floor. Annie Mae was so scared, she told Dalton to take her home to her parents in Potterville, Louisiana (Annie Mae's parents were my soon to be grandparents, Papo and Mamo). Fortunately, Dalton's horse was hitched outside the dance hall.

(Later, my Dad's brother, my Uncle Rene`, referred to my Dad as Lochinvar because he had taken my Mother home from the dance on the back of his horse, just like the Knight Lochinvar in Sir Walter Scott's poem by that name. My Dad did not like the name Lochinvar so my Uncle Rene` called my Dad's horse, Lochinvar.)

Annie Mae's parents had listened to the entire Chase & Sanborn Hour (a Mercury Theatre radio production and broadcast), and they had learned that the Martian invasion was some kind of hoax.

People all over the United States were scared, and they were leaving their homes not knowing at the time that the broadcast was a hoax. People did not know where they were going or what they were going to do. The masses were running to safety. Many people would not learn the truth about the hoax for days or even weeks. People had caught trains, planes, busses, drove their own vehicles, and even walked or ran for miles to hide from the Martians.

Annie Mae (like many other women), was afraid of the news and radio broadcasts from that day forward. The Chase & Sanborn Hour, a major source of family radio entertainment, aired each Sunday evening at 8 p.m., but Mama and many other young women refused to listen to the show. The women did not consider the show's host, Edgar Bergen (and his dummy, Charlie McCarthy) trustworthy. (A few years later, the radio announcement of the Pearl Harbor Attack would do even greater mental harm to women.)

Soon after the Martian radio incident, Dalton (Nole) Sonnier and Annie Mae Louviere` were married (much to the chagrin of Olivia Seymour Sonnier). Ursin Sonnier was amused and happy for my parents. Grandma Sonnier was concerned that Annie Mae, who was a few years older than Dalton, was to mature for her baby boy. (family feud - *querelle de famille* - dysfunctional)

Not long after my parent's marriage, Dalton Joseph Sonnier was drafted into the Army Air Corp. During that time Annie Mae Louviere` Sonnier gave birth to Mervin Joseph Sonnier (my older brother). Mervin contracted measles and a severe fever when he was a few weeks old. The doctor feared for his life. Dalton notified his superiors of this family crisis, provided the necessary medical verification along with a family letter, and the military released him from further service due to family hardship. (Dalton's older brother, Uncle Rene`, had some influence upon the military decision by writing them a letter on behalf of my Mother and Grandma Sonnier.)

The Doctor stated in his accompanying letter that Mervin was extremely ill, possibly near death. Mervin had a difficult time, but pulled through thanks to the constant good care of my Mama, Grandma Sonnier, and my Daddy's sisters.

My Daddy was released from active service duty and returned to Rayne, Louisiana and his family. Less than one month later Mama, Daddy, and Mervin joined the Louviere` family in Biloxi, Mississippi. My Aunt Annie Louviere` Hebert and my Uncle Wilfred (Poncho) Louviere`, my mother's siblings, along with their immediate families traveled to Biloxi and rented houses in the Cajun occupied camps provided for seafood workers (similar to the company houses in mill or coal towns). Papo and Mamo Louviere` and their other children traveled by Greyhound bus to Biloxi to start a new life away from sharecropping and indentured servitude.

Over the years my Mama and Daddy would have three children, my brother Mervin, my sister Judy, and myself Ron. My parents were married over 60 years when Mama died in her early eighties.

I remember Mama often told me, "You don't need that, no. You don't need that." I believe she wanted to protect me from hurt or failure. Mama knew that Cajuns had suffered over the past years and she could not predict the future. I believe she had been held back herself and wanted so many things she thought she could never have. But, sometimes, I did need that.

We Cajuns may have been considered a marginal group, a minority culture at one time, but that has changed. Language, culture, and kinship patterns may well have kept us separate, and we may not have maintained our sense of group identity as we experienced difficulties. It may be accurate to note that Cajun settlement patterns may have isolated us. The Cajun French language did in fact keep us out of the English speaking mainstream. It is also true that the majority of us Cajuns farmed, hunted, and fished, whereas our livelihood hardly required us to assimilate.

Acadian Cajuns settled The Piney Woods forest region and The Gulf Coast of Mississippi. Cajuns of today no longer resemble these remarks not even in the bayous of Louisiana. Incorrect or corrupted history has sought to distort and or undermine our advances in this American Gumbo, sometimes referred to as the Melting Pot and or Salad Bowl, The United States of America.

One way Cajun parents had to assure that they would not experience shunning, ridicule, or failure was to prepare the way for a normalcy and clannish structure staying

24

removed from the overwhelming challenges of main-stream society.

Like a recurring dream, when I desire something (as an example, wanting to purchase an expensive car I do not need), I remember my Mama's voice telling me, "You don't need that, no. You don't need that." I believe that Mama was preparing me to evaluate my needs and desires. I did not especially need certain desired things over the years as I experienced more pressing needs of my family. In the inner recesses of my mind, I continue to hear these same words spoken by my Mama, and I will continue to hear her voice as I sojourn through this life.

I believe parents need to realize that there comes a time when they must, with respect, set their children free to succeed or fail.

Silhouettes - Shadows - and Soft Lights
"et lumieres douces"

I was born in a house (1107 East Beach Street), not a hospital. I was delivered by Dr. Joseph Kuljis and my live birth was documented and certified. My place of birth was Biloxi, Mississippi.

I recall my earliest recollection of my own existence as a human being at about six months of age. I can remember my Mama holding me in a warm blanket and rocking me back and forth in a rocking chair. As Mama rocked, I watched silhouettes and moving shadows that were cast on the walls by soft dim lights. The dim light was cast by a kerosene lamp that hung from a string over our modest kitchen table. The kerosene lamp not only provided light, it was a source of heat for our kitchen.

I recall hearing my Mama and Daddy talking. My parent's voices sounded like a rhythmic song. My parents spoke in their pleasant dialect of broken English and Cajun French. They were talking about how unsafe the kerosene lamps could be and how there had been fires in other houses because of carelessness. "Don't hang the lamp from the ceiling anymore using a string," Mama instructed Daddy, "Sit it in the middle of the table." All the silhouettes, shadows, and soft lights moved about the rooms and settled into their different places, and I felt safer.

Our home was in a place called Sea Coast Camps, *(Ce fut dans un endroit appele camps, Cote de lamer)* which had been built in the salt marshes. We and our neighbors had some semblance of family life, a poor existence; I did not know that we were poor. Life was particularly difficult for the women who were Biloxi's poor, and I witnessed firsthand the hardships my Mama and her sisters and friends suffered in Biloxi.

My next recollection was feeling and knowing that there was something besides me and or us, my family that is. There was someone, or something, I could not see, or put my hands on, but knew was there, near enveloping all of us, and this left me with a feeling of security. I possessed a gentle calmness, peacefulness, and a serenity which I could not explain or comprehend. I did not understand my deep feelings of apprehension and fear of a definite presence of someone, or something, dark and evil, that I could not see, or put my hands on, but knew was there and trying its best to envelop my small family when chaos or troubles came from outside our home and threatened our serenity. I could feel this through the treble in my Mama's and Daddy's voices and their words.

I had this inner peace, I felt protected by a light not from the lamps or the sun, but deep in my little baby boy heart and the very intellect of my soul. Of course, I had not as yet heard of my heart or the intellect of my soul, but I had good feelings. There is something besides all this; I had this feeling at that early age, as a mere baby not long out of my Mama's womb.

I had not as yet experienced the fear of darkness from or during the lunar moon. We were not alone, and I sensed and dearly missed a good someone. Perhaps for the first time in my young life I knew and had a sense of the existence of some dark sinister lunar force. I sensed an occurrence which occupied space and time, for evil purposes, that lurked, as well as slithered about, as did an even more powerful force, that eternal bright light and warm spiritual occupier of elect human souls which I could not comprehend, understand, or even begin to explain of my inner spirit, my free Cajun spirit.

(Cajuns established settlements in the Louisiana-Texas border regions. Texans refer to the triangle of the Acadian Colonies of Beaumont, Port Arthur, and Orange, Texas as Cajun Lapland because that is where the land of Louisiana and Texas lap over into each other. South of the prairies and their waterways is the coastal wetlands. This is one of the most distinctive Cajun regions in North America. This region of Acadian French (Cajun) settlement is central to their image. The culture and seafood cuisine of these Cajuns has represented Cajuns to the world.)

Every night, in our home, the radio was playing music and would be interrupted by Edward R. Morrow with the news, or the radio serials, "The Whistler," or the "Creaking Door." My brother Joe and I were terrified when the whistling or creaking sounds interrupted the quietness of our bedroom. As we squealed from fear and panic, we were in fact delighted with the excitement it generated. My Daddy would say, "You boys had better be quiet..., and "Don't make me come in there." Daddy's comments would cause us to crave his attention, and we would scream until he told us to turn the radio off so that we could get some sleep (we went to sleep at 6:00 p.m. in the evening).

We would listen to both of these radio mysteries well into our teen years, and my Daddy would always have the same reaction at 6:00 p.m. (Daddy rose each morning at 3:00 a.m., Monday through Friday, to go to work at Keesler AFB, he did this for thirty years and retired at age fifty-five due to my Mother's health).

When Edward R. Morrow was on the radio it would get deafeningly quiet in our house and Mama looked really worried as she talked fast, in her Cajun French, to my Daddy. Mama would say let's stay busy, and she would walk back and forth about the kitchen doing different things like opening cabinet doors, but getting nothing out of the cabinets. She was just staying busy, occupying her hands and body to avoid hearing what Mr. Morrow was saying.

At different times, I did sense and know from the aroma emitting from Mama's kitchen that something was cooking. I heard statements like, take the cleaned fresh mullet, oyster, crab, or shrimp, then dip the seafood in eggs and milk (if we had either), toss them in yellow cornmeal that had been seasoned with a little salt and pepper, then place the seafood in the black skillet (cast iron frying pan). The black skillet had hot melted lard in it and the seafood would cook until golden brown and crispy on the outside. This seafood menu was often served in our home along with bread on the side, fresh warm French bread, torn and not cut. We ladled our soft warm bread with mayonnaise and placed our seafood on the bread and folded it into a sandwich.

Mama often made a filet` (a special greenish brown seasoning made from sassafras leaves) okra gumbo. The gumbos were made in various combinations using chicken, *Andouille* sausage (French), crabs, shrimp, and or oysters. My Mama learned to make French dishes and gumbos from her Mama, who learned from her Mama, who passed on the understanding of how to make gumbo from what you had. My Mama had the skill to make a great dark roux (flour and oil mixture cooked until black brown, but not burned), and she knew when to add this ingredient to her gumbo. "Roux is the key she would insist, bad roux, bad gumbo," Mama would say.

Mama would make a potato salad to accompany the gumbo or seafood. She would boil her eggs and potatoes together in the same pot. After determining that the potatoes were cooked, she would cool the potatoes and eggs, then peel the eggs. The eggs were placed in a bowl and mashed with a fork. Salt, pepper and mayonnaise (pronounced, my oh nays) were added to the eggs and all ingredients were mixed to a dressing consistency. After the cooked potatoes were cooled, she would use a butter knife and cut through them to make smaller pieces. Once the potatoes were the correct size, she would gently mix the egg dressing with the potatoes, perfection (my wife, Barbara makes this type of potato salad for me, but it never tasted right until she mixed the ingredients separately, mixing all at once did not produce Mama's potato salad). In my travels around the world, I have encountered this type of potato salad and it is called *Mayonnaise* (my-oh-nays).

Although my Mama had mental illness limitations, she heroically plodded through her life as a wife, mother, and wage earner. Most often I remember her being kind and gentle through it all. Mama was a good valiant soldier. I knew the small nucleus of my family was content at the time, and that my Mama was very smart and a real good cook. Mama would cook many great meals the rest of her kind and gentle life.

My Mama contracted chickenpox as a child in Potterville, Louisiana, the place of her birth. Mama would die, of a heart attack, after her system became weak due to a case of Shingles. Mama was in her eighties when she died in the Ocean Springs Hospital, Ocean Springs, Mississippi. I told my Mama I loved her over and over, many times. *(J'ai dit a ma Maman que je l'aimais encore et encore, de nombreuses fois.)*

My Soulmate

On September 26, 1944, at the very young age of seven months, I realized that something wonderful was taking place, somewhere and somehow beyond my comprehension. On that eventful day, our neighbors the Millers, were having a baby. R. L. Miller, US Navy Ensign (my Daddy's Mate as he called him), was somewhere in the Pacific fighting a war. R. L.'s young wife, Sally Ann Goff Miller, was giving birth to my soulmate, Barbara Ann Miller, in the Biloxi Hospital.

R. L. Miller, his actual given first name, was the son of a keen strong willed business woman of Irish, English, and French (to the best of my knowledge) descent. After R. L.'s birth, Marguerite Teller Miller had moved her family of four boys, by horse drawn wagon, from Picayune, Mississippi to Gulfport, Mississippi, and finally to Biloxi, Mississippi. After arriving in Biloxi, Marguerite opened a bar, guesthouse, or tavern as these local establishments were/are called.

Marguerite Teller Miller was a good decent woman who built clientele by providing food and alcoholic beverages to local fishermen. Marguerite was kind to everyone. Marguerite was known to be a wonderful person, a great cook and housekeeper, and her appearance and mannerisms always reminded me of the redheaded (Marguerite was dark haired) female saloon keeper, Belle Watling in "Gone with the Wind" (the book written by Margaret Mitchell in 1936). Bell Watling was perfectly cast and portrayed in the film version of "Gone with the Wind" by the actress Ona Munson. In the movie, while sitting in a carriage outside her saloon with Mrs. Ashley Wilkes (portrayed by Olivia de Havilland), Bell Watling said to Mrs. Wilkes, "I got a boy myself…….."

John 8:7 King James Version of the Holy Bible *Jesus said, "He that is without sin among you, let him first cast a stone at her."*

I met Marguerite Miller only twice and on both occasions she was very cordial and kind to me. The reputation of her establishment, notwithstanding, she was a good woman, and a magnificent mother to all her children. A man in her line of business would be accepted, but a woman opening a guesthouse, an old local tavern, was considered by the women of Biloxi as being unacceptable. Their husbands would not stay home, but instead chose to drink for long hours, days while waiting for the next shrimp boat to depart the local wharf with fresh ice and salt for the Gulf. The Dixie Café was only one of their havens for escape and drinking.

Marguerite Miller was a great philanthropist and benefactor, as well as, a successful and shrewd businesswoman. Businessmen talked well of her, and well they should have. The wives of some businessmen in Biloxi were jealous, envious rumor mongers of the worst kind, and often had too much time on their hands. Marguerite and other small businessmen and women would help pave the political climate for gambling casinos on the Coast.

All of Marguerite Miller's children and grandchildren would come to know Barbara Ann, the daughter of their youngest brother and uncle, R. L. Miller. The family would know that Barbara Ann was special in the eyes of their matriarch, Marguerite Miller. Marguerite dearly loved Barbara Ann. Barbara Ann Miller had arrived and was a force to be reckoned with.

Barbara used to ride her bike from her home on Bowen Street to her Grandma Miller's residence and business location on Bayview Avenue. During many of those visits, Marguerite would drive Barbara in her big Buick sedan to Evergreen Cemetery in Gulfport, Mississippi, to visit R. L.'s grave. Barbara's mother did not tell her anything about her father (reminds me of the young girl in Bruce Willis' movie, "In Country").

****

The next several months and years would bring hurricanes and family hardships to all the residents of Biloxi, and the entire Gulf Coast.

(Until the beginning of the twentieth century, U.S. corporate culture had relatively little impact on southern Louisiana. The majority of Cajuns did not begin to Americanize until the turn of the twentieth century; several factors combined to quicken the pace. These factors included the nationalistic fervor of the early 1900's followed by World War. Perhaps the most substantial change for Cajuns occurred when big business came to extract and sell southern Louisiana's oil. The discovery of oil in 1901 in Jennings, Louisiana, brought in outsiders and created salaried jobs. This arrangement of historical facts put into words is very common and giving credit is impossible, no infringement intended.)

Hurricane Coming
"L`ouragan Coming"

Another of my earliest memories is from mid-1947 approximately two years from my birth. Somehow, I was aware that a major storm, possibly a hurricane, was approaching the Coast. I sensed the fear growing within the people in my family. The radio played all night as we listened and learned that the tropical depression moved toward the southern tip of Florida. I know, from my firsthand experience, that a child can sense the fear and foreboding emanating from their mothers.

I remember riding on the right hip of a sturdy strong young woman with brown hair, my Taunt Tin Louviere`, wife of my Mama's eldest brother Whitney (Doc) Louviere`. I was straddling Taunt Tin's hip, holding on tightly with my tiny hands, short legs and bare feet. I could hear wind whistling through the cracks in the two-hole outhouses behind every other house. My Mama (who had experienced hurricanes) was yelling to my Taunt Tin that she wished we had some tire tubes. Mama said excitedly, "We need some big truck tire tubes like they tied their kids to when Hurricane King hit Biloxi." "The tubes helped save the Mamas and their kids from being washed out into the Gulf of Mexico," Mama told Taunt Tin.

Maman a dit avec enthousiasme "Nous avons besoin de certains de ces grands tubes de pneus de camion comme ils ont attaché a leurs enfants lorsque l`ouragan a frappe le roi Biloxi. "Les tubes ont aide a sauver les Mamas et leurs enfants d`etre lave dans le golfe du Mexique," Maman dit.

According to my Mama, some years earlier Hurricane King (*roi* is king in French, they were not naming hurricanes at that time, female names were assigned to hurricanes beginning in 1953) had destroyed Biloxi. Mama called the hurricane, *roi*, giving it a name others had called it and not some weather bureau. Every year Mama and the other women would be terrified by news from the radio or from fishermen out in their boats, or from "The Biloxi Daily Herald," or the New Orleans newspaper, "The Times Picayune," reporting strong tropical depressions originating off the coast of Africa and heading toward the outer islands in the Atlantic. Jamaica, the Virgin Islands and then islands in the Caribbean would always be in the direct path and hit first. These islands sometimes slowed the speed of the tropical depression before it entered the Gulf of Mexico. The warm waters of the Gulf promoted strengthening the tropical depressions to hurricane force.

I remember quite well the hurricane that hit the Mississippi Coast in 1947, two years after World War II had ended. The incident of the 1947 hurricane occurred when soldier's bodies were still being returned home to Biloxi. My child remembrance was of a warm salt laced wind spray mixed with rain blowing on my face and naked chest, my feet bare and my middle body dressed only in a pinned white cloth diaper. I remember my fear, a tremendous fear. My little legs were wrapped around the right side of Taunt Tin's waist, just above her hip, and my hands clutched her blouse. I was terribly afraid, but of what I did not know or comprehend as I trembled.

The 1947 hurricane first hit Miami, Florida as a category four and passed through into the Gulf of Mexico in the middle of September. On September 19, 1947 the storm hit the Coast of Mississippi and the Louisiana islands as a category three hurricane. The tide was about twelve feet at Biloxi, Gulfport, and Bay St. Louis, Mississippi. Our families were well prepared.

Staying closely tucked to my Taunt Tin was the customary way I spent my day. Sometimes my Aunt Gurt Louviere`, another close family helper, took care of us while my Mama and most of the Louviere` family worked on fisher boats, shrimp boats (as they were called), or shucked oysters or picked shrimp in the factories to earn money. They worked hard to scrape some cash together (very minimal pay, but it was work), like most of the other women in Sea Coast Camps and Grego's Camps. These camps housed factory workers and other poor working class people. The camps were made available for rent to the workers by the various local factories (similar to coal and mill town communities, to my knowledge there were no company stores).

The houses were square with two bedrooms, a kitchen and living room. There was a front porch that extended across the entire front of each house. Each house had been built on cinder blocks with a three foot crawl space beneath the houses. The crawl spaces of the houses were wrapped in tin that was nailed around the entire periphery of each frame house. (The tin wrapping was the same material that factory roofs and sides were constructed with.) The tin underpinning was to protect the houses and keep them from blowing away during high winds.

My Mama, like most other women, frequently had to depend on The Sisters of Mercy, of St. Michael's Church, for infant care. The factory women of Biloxi had it extremely hard both mentally and physically. The Shrimp Pickers and or Oyster Shuckers *(Le Sélecteur de crevettes est, et ou Oyster Shucker de)* as they were called would wake early every morning, about 3:00 a.m., and carry their infants to the Sisters at the convent. The Sisters would care for the children until about six o'clock a.m. when they would open the Holy Angels Nursery for other mothers and their babies.

Sometime later ..... *(Quelque temps plus tard...)*

R. L. was My Daddy's Mate
"R. L. Mate etait mon papa"

Though just a child and not yet out of diapers, I knew of Barbara's existence. I remember my Mama and Daddy speaking of R. L. and Sally Ann Miller's baby girl's birth. On one occasion, I heard my Mama and Daddy saying sadly that R. L., my Daddy's Mate (Sally's young husband and Barbara's natural Father) would not come home from the war. R. L. had died from wounds received while fighting on a Pacific Island.

R. L. was a very industrious hard working young man of Irish, English and French descent. R. L. was very handsome with curly black hair, an olive complexion and hazel eyes. He was lean, six feet in height, with broad shoulders, long legs and big hands with long pianist fingers.

R. L. had been shot in his left side while on a Japanese occupied volcanic island in the Pacific. R. L. had been cared for, as best they could manage in those days, by US Marine Medics. R. L. died on May 6, 1945 of complications from his wound.

According to Sammy Miller, his brother, while R. L. was a youngster he had his own small businesses. He was a shoe shine boy and would hop aboard trains when they stopped at the station in Biloxi and shine passengers shoes (R. L. would be ever alert to the departing train whistle so that he could hop off the train before it started again). R. L. would also buy seafood early each morning off of seafood boats and go door to door and sell his wares. R. L. was quite smart and very industrious. Before R. L. went into the Navy he worked on seafood boats and was a Barq's Root Beer route driver (he delivered the beverage to various businesses around Biloxi). Yes, he did build those small businesses.

R. L. Miller, a World War II hero who gave all, was and is grandfather to my children Scarlett Lynn Sonnier, born July 3, 1963 at the US Army Hospital in Wurzburg, Germany; Bryan Keith Sonnier, born February 10, 1965 in Biloxi, Mississippi; Sean Christopher Sonnier, born May 3, 1966 in Biloxi, and Darren Ashley Sonnier, born December 1, 1968 in Biloxi.

Special acknowledgement should be taken of J. T. Miller, Sr. (Sammy), R. L.'s older brother. Sammy was a fisherman and master boat builder. Barbara told me that her Uncle Sammy was a talented artist, and we both know him to be a very special person.

During these war days, I could sense the terror, the very trembling in the bodies of the women in my life and I knew that there was something foreboding, dark and sinister lurking in the world. I sensed that we were the good in this world, and that somehow we would prevail (I could not think in these words, but I had deep feelings. Children have acute senses). I had a sense that my Mama and Sally Ann Miller, Barbara's mother, were mentally shattered by hardships and the terrors war brought to their lives.

Neighbors rumored that you could hear Sally's screams for blocks around their home on Hoxie Lane when the military came to solemnly announce that her husband R. L. had been killed in action. Sally Ann Miller was a broken woman; broken to the very fabric of her being. A once reasonably happy young woman was now mentally destroyed, never to recover from the mental and emotional devastation. Sally Ann would become more dependent on her Mama (Barbara's Maw maw), and her child, Barbara Ann Miller, through the ensuing years.

I envision the scene several years later at the Biloxi Train Depot, R. L.'s family and loved ones there to meet his coffin. (Many of the military remains were returned for several years after World War II ended.) Barbara told me that she could remember going to the train depot and seeing a wooden caisson rolled to a freight car door and a flag draped coffin placed on the caisson. (In all likelihood R. L.'s body returned to Biloxi on one of the trains that he had shined shoes on as a young entrepreneur.)

Barbara also told me that she does not remember a lot from her childhood, but she vividly remembered that event, she also remembered being in the Bradford-O'Keefe viewing room and seeing people and the flag draped coffin. People were visiting while having coffee and donuts, and she recalled that days later she was driven to The Evergreen Cemetery in Gulfport. Barbara told me she remembered hearing the Honor Guard gun salute.

Over the years Barbara told me that she had no idea how old she was when R. L. was returned to the states. She told me that she could not possibly have been a baby. A few years before her Daddy (Carl Simmons) died Barbara asked Carl how old she was at the time of R. L.'s funeral. Carl told Barbara that she was about five years old. Carl was at the train station, along with his wife, Sally Ann Goff Miller Simmons, Sally's mother Evelyn Waltman Goff (Maw maw), and Barbara's Grandma Miller (Marguerite Teller Miller, R. L.'s Mother). Barbara said she thought that other Miller family members were there, but did not know who.

When Barbara had been born, her Grandma Miller (Marguerite) had wanted to name Barbara Margaret (spelled differently than her own name), but Sally Ann and Evelyn Goff refused.

I can think about and even see the long black train, see the steam, and hear the whistles blowing mournfully. The trains participated in a solemn duty, and they were magnificent in those days.

As though in a vivid dream, when I think about those events I can see Barbara very clearly. Barbara is wearing a pretty dress (dressed by her Maw maw because she lived with her and not with her Mama and new Daddy Carl). I can see a navy blue taffeta dress with pink polka dots, trimmed in pink lace. She wore black patent leather shoes and a bow in her raven black curly hair. I picture hair so black it had that deep dark blue hue, like a ravens feathers (her coloring: skin, hair and eyes like her father R. L.). Barbara had been led, by her Mother, to believe that R. L. had blond hair and hazel blue eyes (the coloring of his navy picture that was in a large oval frame).

Sally could be a very sweet lady (she was a beautiful lady), but she could when putting on a syrupy type talk hide her conniving disagreeable side. At times she was one mixed up lady arguing with her own mother, and or Barbara Ann (as Sally called Barbara, not showing her any affection). Sally withheld the love of a mother, which Barbara craved, and doled that love out to Barbara's siblings (the others) while taunting and pushing Barbara's affections aside like garbage.

Like my Mama many of the women had menopause, mid-life crisis, and or Post-Partum Depression (a phenomenon at that time not yet diagnosed or adequately explained causing mental and physical ailments with occasional outbursts of violent temperament, sometimes requiring treatment and or even hospitalization). My Mama's major lifelong debilitating illness was jealousy; this jealousy led to social issues. Mama could become violent and strike out at even her best friends, but never her children (she even struck out at her innocent friend and neighbor, Letty Illich).

Throughout many years, Letty was a true friend to our family, and my Mama's patient understanding neighbor and truest friend. We children, myself, my brother Mervin, and my sister Judy, loved Letty, she was like a second Mama to us. Our family called Letty by her given name that is what she preferred. Letty was totally loyal to my Mama.

Dr. K and others would prescribe valium and other anti-depression prescription drugs to Biloxi women. These doctors would quite often perform hysterectomies in large numbers in the Deep South. These procedures were immensely profitable and thought to control the upset women. Perhaps in most cases valium and or a hysterectomy was sound medical alternatives to that of a life of mental anguish for the female and her family (second guessing doctors years later about these actions is not productive or proper, the doctors did their best, I am sure).

The war (World War II) had been extremely hard on women and particularly on wives and mothers who lost husbands, loved ones, sons and daughters. These women would suffer a wound that hurt until their own passing.

Marguerite Miller never accepted R. L.'s death. She believed that her youngest son was missing in action or perhaps a POW (Prisoner of War). Marguerite received misleading letters from the War Department confusing the status of her son, missing or killed. She hired private investigators and hounded the US Navy until her death in 1961. Marguerite was laid to rest in the family plot which she purchased in Evergreen Cemetery, Gulfport, Mississippi. She purchased this plot to be near her parents, Joseph and Anise Teller and her son, R. L.

Over fifty years after R. L.'s death, his only child Barbara would write to The US Navy and Veterans Administration for a copy of his military records. R. L. Miller had returned home to Biloxi and it was a verifiable fact that it was his remains in the decorated casket and not merely rocks as his brother Sammy Miller had been cruelly told. (It was the custom after the war to place rocks in an empty casket for burial if there were no actual remains.) I was with Barbara and Sammy when she told him she had copies of R. L.'s military records and that she would mail copies to him. The look of comfort on his face cannot be described.

Well, there were remains, and R. L. had died a hero and was held in the loving arms of his brothers the, Seabees of Gulfport, Mississippi, the US Navy, and the Marine Medical Corp, to be returned to his family (his mother Marguerite, his widow Sally Ann and his daughter, Barbara Ann) in Biloxi, Mississippi.

It is worth repeating and clarifying that there are no rocks in the coffin of a Biloxi favorite son. Navy Ensign R. L. Miller was not missing in action; he was never a POW. R. L. Miller had for a fact died of wounds from a Japanese soldier's sniper rifle and was returned to Biloxi, Mississippi. His flesh body was buried in Evergreen Cemetery, Gulfport, Mississippi and returned to the soil even as his eternal spiritual body and soul is with his mother Marguerite in Paradise and with the God of Abraham, Isaac and Jacob.

Abe

Abe Goff, younger and only brother of Sally Ann Goff Miller, was another of R. L. Miller's best friends and brother-in-law. Abe was to become quite a legend in his life time. This legend began when an accident occurred on the old Biloxi to Ocean Springs Bridge. A milk truck driver had swerved to miss a dog while driving on the bridge. The truck hit and crashed through the guard rail of the bridge and was hanging through the cement rail over the water twenty feet below. The accounts given by witnesses and family are that Abe (in his bare feet) had been fishing on the side of the bridge when he saw the accident. Abe immediately assessed what needed to be done and rushed over to help.

Abe later told the police that the desperate man was banging his fists on the inside of the door and the front windshield of the Borden's milk truck. As Abe was assessing the driver's plight, the truck continued to slide slowly toward the water. Neither Abe nor the truck driver had time to wait for help. Abe determined from the driver's efforts to get out that the doors would not open and that the driver was stuck inside.

Witnesses told of how Abe grabbed hold of the back bumper and tried to pull the truck back onto the bridge proper. The truck would not budge as it was wedged between concrete rail pillars. The bridge side pillars were about four feet in height and about one foot square. Some observers tried to help Abe, but they were scared of going over the edge with the truck. Abe calmly and softly told them that they were only in his way. During this time, the truck continued to slip, and its downward movement made squealing and screeching sounds on the bridge concrete.

Cars and trucks began stopping, and traffic blocked the bridge on both sides. No traffic moved as people left their vehicles and walked tentatively toward the crowd. They could see other spectators pointing excitedly toward the impending disastrous scene.

Abe moved to the middle of the back bumper on the truck to try and halt the sliding, but this did not help. He then moved to the front left side of the truck, grabbed hold of the truck again and lifted the truck a couple of feet freeing the front tire as he moved it backwards a small amount. Abe had managed to change the position of the truck enough to pull the truck back about a foot or two. Once there was working room, Abe with his back to the water below gave a mighty grunt and lifted the heavy front end high enough to free the passenger side front tire and move the truck forward and onto the bridge proper. The crowd had watched in awe and told the police that it was a super human thing that Abe Goff had done.

Eye witnesses said that Abe hammered the driver's doors (double folding doors) with the palms of his huge hands and then charged into them with his massive shoulder forcing an opening large enough for him to insert his thick strong fingers and pull the doors open. Abe tore the doors off the hinges freeing the man that had been trapped.

The eye witnesses reported that the man in the milk truck never moved from his seat the entire time Abe was trying to free him from the slipping truck and certain drowning. They also told of how Abe grabbed the man, cradled him in his arms, then hoisted him to his shoulder and carried the rather large man to safety some twenty feet away from the truck. This is when The Legend of Big Abe Goff (at that time still a young man) began and grew as he would turn into a gentle kind giant (Giant Oak Tree Adorned With Spanish Moss), a family man, and a very special beloved uncle.

Abe would perform similar superhuman adrenalin rush feats over his life time continuing to earn the unplanned unsolicited legend for himself.

Abe and his wife Yvonne (a very close friend to his sister Sally Ann) eventually moved to Louisiana. The couple reared three sons (R. L., Roland and Noland) and three daughters (Jerry, Mary and Lesha). Their first born son was named after his Uncle R. L. Miller, and he grew to be a six foot six inch gentle, soft spoken giant of an athletic man. R. L. was just like his Daddy Abe. Yvonne's and Abe's other two sons were twins, Roland and Noland. They were about five foot ten inches in height and had moderate body frames. Roland and Noland were also gentle and soft spoken like their Dad. The girls were all lovely and well-mannered similar to their mother Yvonne. They were also gentle like Abe.

Abe and Yvonne were known for helping men find jobs. Aunt Yvonne stood about five foot nine or ten inches tall. She had broad shoulders, long legs (Amazon type woman), and her hair was blonde and wavy. Aunt Yvonne had a sweet southern accent, another southern bell, and would take people that needed help into their home for weeks and sometimes months at a time until a job was secured. (Yvonne made the world's best home-made biscuits.)

Over the years, Abe would return home to Biloxi to visit family. Abe's children loved to visit the coast, but Abe did not like Biloxi's crime syndicate atmosphere. Abe loved to bring his children to Biloxi for a few days visit, but looked forward to the return trip to Alexandria where his entire family loved living.

Abe helped find work in the oil field for his brother-in-law, Carl Simmons. Carl always remembered Abe helping him. Carl and Abe became the very best of friends and they had great respect for each other. Carl worked many years for Williams Oil Drilling Company out of Golden Meadow, Louisiana.

Abe worked for many years in the offshore oilfields of Louisiana and Texas in the Gulf of Mexico waters. Abe's family lived in Elizabeth and later moved to Alexandria, Louisiana. They loved Alexandria and Alexandria loved them. In addition to Abe's oil field years in the Gulf of Mexico waters, he would take his family with him to foreign ports including The North Sea (Norway) and Trinidad.

Abe would work as a Deep-water Driller. Abe's own sweat (saltier due to salt tablets for excessive heat and sweating out body salt) caused an inner ear problem that would affect his hearing for the rest of his life. Abe after many years left the oil fields and tried his hand at a small business of cutting and selling timber. He purchased his own truck and equipment. Yes, he did build that.

One night while sleeping in his bed which was next to a wall, Abe got his feet entangled in the sheets. Abe twisted and in a daze, half asleep, he kicked out ferociously at the sheets and struck the wall with his bare foot. The wall did not give and his toes were traumatized. Abe had diabetes and unbeknownst to him (not considering this accident serious), the accident would cause his toe, foot, and then leg to become inflamed with gangrene.

Abe's injury and subsequent onset of gangrene led to the amputation of his left leg below the knee. Abe would muster his usual courage, utilize a cane and move forward in life like the champion of a giant (Giant Oak Tree Adorned With Spanish Moss) that he was. Abe passed away at the relatively young age of 73. He was extremely well regarded and loved by everyone who knew him, including me.

The Alligator That Barked
"L`alligator qui aboyait"

Under the canopy of the partially clear blue morning skies and the cloud filled afternoon skies (cumulus white clouds came in from the Gulf of Mexico in the afternoons), there were the frequent rain showers which brought fresh clean water to sustain an abundance of living creatures in the continuous life cycle on the Coast. The foliage and vegetation in the salt marsh was sporadic being both sparse and thick on either side of the numerous trails and or paths behind the Sea Coast Camps houses. These marshes with their numerous trails and paths led all the way to the factories, piers, wharfs, and docks. The trails and paths were quite near and adjacent to where I lived, across a section of marsh in sight of seafood factories.

As I walked along the various paths, I could see numerous species of birds. The birds were in abundance on the sandy marsh ground, on the sandy beach, in the Gulf of Mexico's warm salty waters, in the air, perched on wires, and on glass balls affixed to the cross beams of telephone poles. The birds on the poles could hear buzzing, and they seemed to sense danger. The birds could feel a vibration of an otherwise undetectable energy that they respected with due caution.

There were rather large pelicans, gulls, terns, herons, egrets, ibises, storks, ducks, geese, the territorial hawks, and the rarely seen evasive and elusive eagles. There were the grayish brown colored small sparrows that lighted everywhere. Robins, mockingbirds, blue jays, willets, sandpipers, rails, plovers, wrens, blackbirds, crows, and skimmers were all in their own paradise on this Biloxi Peninsula.

Squirrels, rabbits, and even wild pigs were there inhabiting the peninsula and nearby Deer Island, Horn Island, and Cat Island. Hunting in Biloxi proper was not allowed and perhaps the wildlife sensed this as they went about their business seemingly with little concern for normal human activities.

Even as a small child, I had the good sense to see and understand that animals survived on basic instincts. No one had to inform me that animals moved when I made a sudden noise, clapped my hands, or separated the cat-of-nine-tails, marsh bushes and grasses as I walked about their habitat. I remember that when I ran, it surprised me to hear bird's wings flapping in hurried flight. I would see them flying away to escape to some safety higher in the heavens or elsewhere in the bushes or tall grass to get away from man, the intruder. I noticed most birds momentarily sought safe haven in the branches, leaves, and moss of the Giant Oak Trees Adorned With Spanish Moss. The Oaks were numerous in Biloxi and could be seen the entire length of the Gulf Coast along Old Highway 90.

One morning in July, I opened the front screen door of our house in Sea Coast Camps and stepped out onto the porch letting the screen door slam behind me. (The wooden front door was always open allowing the Gulf breezes to pass through our house. The breezes flowed to and through the open back screened door. The fresh air passed through the open windows also.) As the door slammed, I expected to hear my Mama call out, "Don't slam the door, this is not a barn," but she said nothing. I walked onto the porch and sat down with my feet on the top step of the porch steps.

As I turned toward the south to look toward the Gulf waters, I saw only sky and an empty lot. I then turned to my left and to the north looking toward Old Highway 90 and the entrance to Sea Coast Camps. At the housing entrance, I saw a black haired barefoot young boy walking with a black and white spotted dog.

One evening I was in my front yard trying to play with the black and white spotted dog, and my Mama shouted from the kitchen in back of the house, "Gumbo!" (Mama calling gumbo meant that our meal was ready). The dog ran and jumped, cleared the steps onto the front porch sliding to the front door expecting some gumbo. From that moment on my Mama and I called the dog Gumbo. When we would call the name Gumbo, he would always come to us.

On another day, I saw Gumbo walking next to a boy (I did not know if it was the boy I saw before with Gumbo), and I was stunned that the dog was so calm. He was walking next to the boy as though they were best friends. I knew this to be one mean dog. I had tried my best to treat him with kindness. I had even given him a name so that he could be my very own first pet dog. I wondered what name the boy called him.

The dog probably would not agree that he liked me, but any time a grownup was around me or other kids, he would get between the kids and grownups and me and growl. When the dog growled, he bared his teeth and the hair would stand straight up on the back of his neck. I thought Gumbo looked like that dog in "Spanky and Our Gang," and or "The Little Rascals." Those dogs were black and white with a black circle, target, around one eye.

Gumbo was just a castaway dog that lived in our neighborhood. The dog barked at everyone except the black haired boy. Gumbo especially barked at my Daddy when he was riding his bike to and from work at Keesler Field. Daddy would whip his hammer out of the holster on his hip, just like a cowboy drawing his six-shooter, and I was always impressed as he waved it at Gumbo. My Daddy called Gumbo, *Chien* (the French word for dog was *Chien*), and other things I did not understand. I could see that Gumbo did not like the words that my Daddy shouted at him. Gumbo seemed to understand the name *Chien*, and he understood my Daddy's hand signals.

No one claimed the dog, but everyone tossed him scraps from their table. Gumbo ignored the scraps as though he had better food elsewhere. Gumbo did not like anyone, nor did he make friends with any of us. Gumbo seemed to love barking at night whether there was a full moon or not. Gumbo loved to bark every night.

Gumbo was feared by all of us kids. He would yap and sometimes growl and nip at our heels while he was jumping back and forth at us and around us. I kind of liked the dog, but I felt he had no particular affection for me. Gumbo would sometimes get between Daddy and me and growl at Daddy. Gumbo jumped back and forth and barked crazily when my Dad passed him. Daddy hardly noticed the dog as he walked by him.

You could hear neighbors talking in threatening tones about Gumbo, but they continued to feed him. The neighbors complained most about his barking. The mutt would bark all night, every night. Daddy and our neighbors yelled out telling him to shut up. No matter how much Gumbo was yelled at he continued to stay in our neighborhood.

Gumbo was a Biloxi Traveling Spirit, a Biloxi Sojourner Spirit, and I respected him for it. Of course, I did not know any of these descriptive words then, but I sensed the spirit of Gumbo to be somewhat like my own. My spirit desired to eventually travel. I did not know then that Gumbo, with his bravery under fire, his excitement, high spirit and almost manic behavior would help me to survive later on in life. I really liked Gumbo *(Chien)*.

On another morning in July, I opened the back screen door of my safe house letting the door slam back on its hinges expecting a harsh rebuke from my Mama. I expected to hear my Mama shout at me, "This is not a barn." *(Oui, nous avons fait construire ce.)* I walked away from the back door for a walk about to explore the great outdoors.

I could see The Ice House and one of the many factories across from our Sea Coast Camps home. I continued walking toward the seafood factories. There was a marshland with a sandy bottom filled with cat-of-nine-tails. The cat-of-nine-tails waved in the breeze blowing in from The Gulf of Mexico. The Gulf was only a short block from my house.

On my walk about, I walked through the marsh vegetation which reached to the top of my sun bleached cotton top head. I could see through and over some of the blades. The blades looked like tall wide blades of grass. I continued down some paths heading for the water. After a short time, I came upon a hole (similar to a military foxhole, as I recall now) in the sandy earth. The hole was about eight feet in diameter and about two feet deep. There was a mound of sand evenly distributed around the perimeter of the hole (I could see Phil D on a hill behind me).

I climbed over the mound of sand which circled the hole and stood in the hole looking all around. All of a sudden, I was startled out of my thoughtfulness by the sound of a voice. The voice was deep, but it was a feminine little girl's voice. The girl's voice was saying to me, "Alligator's dug this hole to lay their babies eggs. Sometimes they lay twenty or thirty eggs at one time." The girl continued, "The fishermen told me about the alligators and their eggs. They said the alligators usually come here in June or July." As she recounted what the fishermen had told her, the little girl said it as though she had witnessed the event many times.

"The alligators come here at night after all the lights are out and it is dark and quiet. They come after we have gone to bed," she told me. The girl said, "They try to get to the pigs and their troughs of food. My family is raising pigs in those pens over there (she pointed at the pig pens)." This little girl was the first person to tell me about alligators.

I stood there watching and listening to the little girl in disbelief (I was wearing my imaginary six guns and holster, while pulling at the real red and gold cowboy bandana that my Daddy had given me so that I could play Cowboys and Indians, I was never without my get-up). I was surprised that she could sneak up on me the way she had. I was always alert to Indians. I was very impressed with the little girl and her ability to move about the marsh quietly.

What she told me about the alligators coming around our houses explained why Gumbo howled and barked so much at night. I stuttered and stammered and finally got words out of my mouth. I asked the girl, "What are you doing here?" *Jai begaye, et begaye, et balbutia et a finalement obtenu mots de ma bouche en disant: "Que faites-vous ici?"* "How did you sneak up on me?" I asked. *"Comment avez-vous faufiler sur moi?"* The little girl replied, "I understand what you are saying to me, isn't that something?" *"Je comprends ce que vous me dites, n'est-ce pas quelque chose?"*

The little girl had a pale face, blue eyes and reddish blonde hair. She was about three feet tall (her feet were bare of shoes like mine), and she had the stature of a giant with her hands on her hips and her bare feet spread shoulder width. Her stance conveyed personal physical strength and status in our community. The girl left no room for doubt as she rambled on and told me, "The daddy alligator sometimes eats the eggs and the little gators when the mama leaves the nest to find fish for herself or food for the babies."

"You are the only little boy my size that I have ever been able to talk with that understands me," the little girl said. *"Vous etes le seul garcon peu ma taille que je n`ai jamais pur parler avec qui me comprend, elle ledit."*

It had not occurred to me that we had both been speaking a foreign language, Cajun French. The girl and I occasionally interjected English as we talked. All the Cajun French people that I knew spoke this way every day. My parents, grandparents, aunts and uncles all spoke this dialect. The little girl and I knew that we were good friends and could speak to each other and comprehend, with words and gestures (especially hand gestures and head shakes), what we wanted to convey. I heard barking in the distance but paid no attention to it.

The girl rapidly, just like me, changed languages again, from Cajun French to English, and said, "My name is Lois Hebert (pronounced ay bayer)." Chattering on she told me with her June Allyson (the actress) voice, "They, the alligators, bark sometimes; they sound just like a dog." Lois rambled on and without moving her feet she turned half around and pointed, "I live over there (as she pointed at a house two houses down from my house and closer to Old Highway 90), I've seen you through my window." I heard more barking as Lois reverted back to Cajun French and said, "You've been out here before, and, I have been afraid the gators would get you." *"Vous avez ete ici avat,"* et, *"J`ai eu peur des alligators serait que vous obtenez."*

All of a sudden, we both heard barking and we saw an alligator close by The Ice House loading dock down by the Gulf. The gator was moving toward us while it was chomping on a furry ball. The gator was standing on its big legs with its tail slithering and whipping side to side. The alligator seemed to be barking at us as it moved closer to us.

I knew that The Ice House stored ice and salt and sold it mostly to the shrimp and oyster boats. When the boat owners were planning a shrimp or oyster trip, they would stop by The Ice House and fill the holds in the bottom of their boats with ice. During their trip (that is what a voyage to catch seafood is called), their catch was placed in the holds, iced down, and the catch would stay fresh while they were in the Gulf.

Lois and I laughed nervously, the barking stopped and the gator swallowed and started walking toward us again. The gator raised its head higher as it moved more hastily and ominously toward us. We stopped laughing and looked nervously in Phil D's direction, but he had left. (Phil D had been standing on an oyster shell hill not far from us.) "Ronnie, let's get out of here," I heard Lois shout. *"Rhone`, J'ai entendu crier Lois, sortons d'ici."*

I looked back to where Lois was supposed to be standing, but she was not there. Lois was tearing through the marsh already far ahead of me. Neither of us hesitated as we made space between us and the alligator. We were both running with swift little legs and bare feet pumping. We did not seem to be making much progress although our feet were slicing through the sand and dense salt marsh. Our feet carried us on our separate paths to our houses. I looked back toward Lois' path and stumbled and fell to my knees. I raised myself as I moved forward, at what I thought was a great speed, but Lois was already at her house. Lois was so fast that I felt like I was standing still. She is a girl I thought, this is very embarrassing.

I thought that I could run fast, but Lois had left me behind. Her speed had made a lasting impression that I was not to forget. Seeing her run had taught me that I was not as fast as I had once thought. I would from that time forward have a more realistic understanding of my abilities and limitations. I came to an understanding that I was not the most gifted athlete in my neighborhood or in Biloxi.

I finally reached the back of my house and stood on our back steps looking for Lois, then for Phil D, but they were gone. Both kids had literally and physically disappeared, each to their own safe haven. I had wet my pants; I thought how embarrassing. With fear, a new found feeling, I looked back again for our gator and saw it slithering down a bank into the Gulf water.

Later that day, I remember my Daddy arrived home on his bike. As he picked the bike up in his arms and parked it on the front porch he looked puzzled and asked me where Gumbo was. Suddenly, I reflected on the morning remembering Lois Hebert, the alligator, and the black and white squirming lump with legs that was in the alligator's jaws. As the alligator had chewed the barking had diminished, became a whimper, and then no sound.

"The Alligator That Barked" was not an alligator barking, it had been our neighborhood protector Gumbo barking. "Oh no," I thought, that must have been Gumbo. *("Oh non," pensais-je, qui doit avoir ete Gumbo.)*

"That alligator ate him, he ate him for sure," I said to my Daddy, and I cried. *"Ce crocodile a mange, il a nabge ciyo sur, j'aid it a mon pere, et j'ai pleure."* "Poor Gumbo," I repeated. "That alligator ate him," I told my Daddy once more. "That alligator ate my Gumbo," I said, as I sobbed uncontrollably.

My Daddy stood there very amused, and he bent over at the waist laughing. Daddy was dressed in his customary work clothes, gray short sleeved shirt, long gray pants, and his gray hat cocked upward on his forehead (like Edward G. Robinson, as Rico, in the film "Little Caesar"). Daddy shook his head back and forth as he laughed. Daddy laughed at me, as he said, "Cowboy, you sure can tell good stories."

"Thank you I thought," I love telling stories. *"Merci, je pensais," J'aime raconteur des histories."* Daddy called me Cowboy because he knew I really liked playacting like I was Hop-a-Long Cassidy (my holster and guns were imaginary).

Daddy told our neighbors my story, and later I heard him tell my uncles. My uncles did not laugh about Gumbo and the alligator that ate him. My uncles started talking very fast in French and broken English (Cajun French).

I learned a few days later, that the alligator had not been a day dream. Once more I opened the screen door of my safe house, letting the door slam back on its hinges. I expected the accustomed harsh rebuke from my Mama for slamming the door. I looked toward where Lois said she lived, no Lois, and then I looked toward where I had last seen Phil D (I realized at that point that the day before Phil D had been standing on one of the numerous oyster shell piles that were as big as our house).

King of the Hill is what the neighborhood boys called the person that would stand on the oyster shell piles. My brother Mervin often participated in King of the Hill. I realize now that when I saw Phil D standing on the oyster shell pile with his legs spread and his hands on his hips that he had looked like a miniature version of the main character in Ayn Rand's book, "The Fountainhead." (Gary Cooper had starred in the movie version of "The Fountainhead," and in the movie he had stood on top of the skyscraper that he was building and his pose was just like Phil D's, legs spread and hands on his hips. Totally in charge and satisfied with himself.)

I peered as best I could in the direction of the seafood factories and the dock attached to it that reached into the Gulf of Mexico. The wharf was more than fifty feet long and came to a tee at the end. Each branch of the tee was about twenty feet or so long. At the end of the wharf there was a great calamity as approximately eight men struggled with what looked to me, from a distance of eight house lengths, to be a giant alligator. The alligator appeared to be eight or ten feet long, and it had a large hook protruding from its huge mouth (the hook was about half an inch thick and very long, because about six inches of the hook protruded from the alligator's huge mouth).

The gator was spinning and thrashing in place. The alligator whipped his huge, thick, pointed, scaly tail as his entire body became more entangled by a long thick rope. The gator's mouth had rope wrapped and knotted around it. His mouth was secured firmly so that he could not open it and bite his captors. Two of my uncles were with the men, and they all jumped around staying clear of the whipping tail. The men were using extremely salty language as they whooped and fought the gator. This scene scared me and for many days I refused to leave our house. My Daddy did not believe that the alligator ate Gumbo, but I never saw *Chien* again.

Looking back to the day when Lois and I met by the alligator hole I remember that I saw, off in the distance behind us and toward Old Highway 90, a young boy watching every move we made. The boy seemed very reticent and bashful, but projected a foreboding appearance as he watched the Gulf and us. The boy acknowledged our presence with an occasional side glance as though waiting for the tragedy of a play to unfold.

This young boy was one spooky character. I remember Lois and I chose to look up at the factory roof and the pelicans resting there and not at the boy. Lois and I continued searching about for more pelicans sitting on the pilings that were just off shore. I knew that Lois could see the boy, but she would not acknowledge his presence. Lois would occasionally look tentatively in his direction. Lois and I had looked away from him and tried to ignore his seemingly creepy presence.

I remembered that I had seen him on other occasions when trouble was afoot and someone would inevitably get hurt, and or even die. I called him by the name others had given him, Phil D. Phil D was at times a bitter young boy. He was small in stature, had a dark sinister charisma, and I sensed and observed others of larger stature (boys older than he) being cautious around him, they feared him. Later as a teenager, Phil D would lose a leg, at the knee, from some freak accident (chopping wood with an axe for his fireplace, I think).

Phil D had some associates, but no close friends. People only tolerated Phil, each for their own personal reason(s). One such associate was my brother Joe (Mervin Joseph Sonnier), and a couple of Joe's friends. Phil D was their age, but I believe it was not Phil D that they most feared, but something dark and troubling around him, something that accompanied his presence.

Years later, Phil D was a person of interest in the murder of a Ms. Hightower (sister of Jenny Hightower, my St. Michaels' classmate) and her boyfriend in Ocean Springs, Mississippi. The murder occurred at The Indian Totem Pole, a parking place for young lovers. While sitting in a car, the young lovers had been shot in their open mouths with a 22 caliber pistol (no fingerprints, other than the victims, were found at the scene or on the gun).

I believe that there was a Guardian Angel protecting Lois and I on the day that we met and talked about alligators. I would not see Lois again for ten years. Over the years I learned to like Phil D. Phil D died at a very young age.

Old Highway 90 was very narrow and had few pullover locations or entrances to the beach. On one particularly pitch black night (no glow from the moon or stars) disaster struck young Phil D. Phil D and four friends had stopped to change a tire on Old 90. The five young men were struck from behind by another car, all were killed.

When struck down, the five young men were all standing behind the car, not knowing that they obstructed the rear lights from the sight of oncoming motorists. They were all hit full force by a vehicle going some sixty miles an hour (brakes were never engaged). My brother Joe had finished high school and enlisted in the US Navy or he would have been with the group. After Joe joined the Navy his best friend, Darryl Satterfield, joined with the small pact of young men and was killed that fateful night.

Phil D already had a criminal record at the time of this tragic accident. His record was of minor nature, but he had received notoriety as a person of interest in the previously mentioned murder investigation. It was learned that Phil D had been a previous boyfriend of the deceased Hightower girl. Moon and one or two other Pointe Cadet boys had also been her friends and most recent beaux's.

Jealousy was considered a possible motive in the murders. The unknown assailant was never found. The Police considered murder suicide. The dead boy possibly murdered the girl and then committed suicide. No motive for the murders was ever discovered. The only fingerprints on the gun were those of the victims. Law enforcement, at the time, considered a traveling bum or possibly an airman from Keesler Air Force Base in Biloxi. There were no clues and the murder and or suicide remains a mystery to this day.

There were no clues and no evidence of an intruder. The car was locked from the inside with the windows rolled up. It was as though some phantom or spirit had committed the crime and left no signs of having ever been present.

That alligator ate my Gumbo. These thoughts remain with me even today.

Clarice

On one of many sojourn escapades from my house in Sea Coast Camps, I walked across Old Highway 90 to Rossetti's Café at the mouth of Back Bay and the Biloxi Ocean Springs Bridge. As I walked past the front of Rossetti's, I looked in the glass windows at customers enjoying their oyster, shrimp or crab po'boys and other seafood items. Oblivious to danger from traffic, I was always traveling through the jungle barefoot like Boy, the son of Tarzan (Tarzan of book and movie fame). I was looking for some new thing or experience.

After I passed Rossetti's I continued on Howard Avenue. I walked two blocks and turned left as I continued on my sojourn. On my right was the front of St. Michael's gym and the Neal Natalich house was on my left. I was stopped dead in my tracks by Police Officer Vanlee. Officer Vanlee was greatly respected by all the kids on The Pointe. We all believed him to be tough but fair. The police officer grilled me thoroughly, third degree questioning, and he finally released me (I thought he might put me in jail, but he did not).

Once released from custody, I moved on toward St. Michael's School. At this point, I was looking south toward the Gulf. In the distance I could see De Jean's (pronounced day john's) Seafood Packing Plant on the Gulf side of Old Highway 90. I then turned left onto 1st Street. On my right, a boy named Poskie lived on the opposite corner. I continued my safari as Boy, the Son of Tarzan, and noted that the jungle in this area was very familiar to me. Very soon, however, my imagination reverted to my Hop-a-Long Cassidy persona, holster and guns, all imaginary. I was completing the circle walking behind Grego's Camps, heading back toward Sea Coast Camps by way of the Holy Angels Nursery and Kindergarten.

Holy Angels was run by Sister Adrian of the Sisters of Mercy of The Immaculate Conception. The Nuns (as they were also known) wore white habits, black full length dresses tied at the waist with a very long black leather belt. The belt hung menacingly from their waist and had a long tongue that extended down to their knees.

I walked down 1st Street heading east behind Grego's Camps to the Holy Angel's Nursery. The nursery was on my right at the very next corner. I could see St. Michael's church steeple peeking above the "Giant Oak Trees Adorned With Spanish Moss."

The Sisters of Mercy had a merry-go-round and other toys in their front yard under their giant oak trees. The Sisters sat on the big front porch saying their Rosary while watching the children who had been placed in their care. I felt for some reason that I liked it there with the Sisters of Mercy, but I knew that I had to sneak around to play on the merry-go-round with the other kids, and so that is what I did, I snuck in. I did not understand why I was not part of this bunch of lucky kids.

There was a little black headed boy on the merry-go-round motioning and calling to me. "Jump on," he said. "Jump on," he called again. The merry-go-round was moving around and around at a fast clip when I jumped onto it with both of my feet finding and standing on the bottom floor. As I landed the boy grabbed me holding onto me and at the same time directing my hands to the chest high metal bars for us to hold on to. "You are brave," the boy said. "I wouldn't have made that jump," he said, and my chest expanded beyond even my belief.

My name is Jackie, Jackie Sherrill," the boy said. "My Brother and I were brought here by Dr. K," he continued. "We own an egg farm," Jackie Sherrill said. He told me that something had happened to his Mama and Daddy and Dr. K and the Sisters were taking care of him and his little brother for now.

The merry-go-round began to slow a little as Jackie stopped prodding and urging it along with his fast legs and feet. Jackie was distracted by Sister Adrian calling to him, "Jackie Sherrill, you slow that thing down." "Jackie, slow down," she warned again. Just then Jackie looked up and toward Sister Adrian and that is when he lost his footing and balance. Jackie went flying through the air onto the dirt of the playground. Jackie hit a couple of large roots as he bounced and slid striking his head on a root and suddenly coming to a horrific stop.

As I jumped off the merry-go-round, Jackie was lying below me (and I thought to myself, Hop-a-Long to the rescue). There were oak tree roots (Giant Oaks Trees Adorned With Spanish Moss) protruding like giant snakes in and out of the ground and Jackie was cradled in them, not moving. Jackie Sherrill was bleeding real blood, a lot of real blood.

I (Hop-a-Long to the rescue) took off my trusted red and gold cowboy bandana and pressed it to Jackie's forehead. Sister Adrian screamed for help and knelt down beside Jackie. For some reason during all the excitement, I realized I was playacting that I was Hop-a-Long Cassidy, and that I was dressed in my customary, though imaginary, Hop-a-Long Cassidy outfit. I thought, "I feel stupid." I had learned from Hop-a-Long and Gabby Hayes that you have to take off your bandana and hold it against a bleeding gunshot wound, and so I had done that.

Jackie started moving, he was trying to get his feet under him, but Sister Adrian held him down. "Don't move yet," Sister Adrian said, over and over with excitement and concern. I was excitedly switching personalities from Hop-a-Long to Boy to Bomba.

Sister Adrian told Jackie that I had saved his life. Sister Adrian said, "Jackie, I believe this little boy saved your life." (My chest pumped out with pride) Then it occurred to me that I was caught. I did not belong on the playground. My imaginary cowboy guns disappeared right before my eyes, and I felt the weight lifted from around my little boy body. They were gone, my guns and holsters were gone. I did not know why I needed to be someone else.

Sister Adrian asked me, "Who are you, what are you doing here?" She then took both of us to the Holy Angel's kitchen. Holy Angel's kitchen was next to the kindergarten on 1st Street behind the Sisters' house. In the kitchen, Sister Adrian nursed us and gave us a big glass of cold tomato juice (Clarice served the tomato juice).

Clarice was a huge (I thought ten times my size as I looked up into her gentle brown eyes) gray haired, very stocky black lady (the first black person I had ever seen). Clarice reminded me of a "Giant Oak Tree Adorned With Spanish Moss." She had a big round face, fat nose and a wonderful genuine smile which exhibited the biggest and prettiest pearly or ivory white teeth that I had ever seen.

Clarice sat us at a table and brought Jackie and me one of the best meals I had ever eaten. On the plate were creamy mashed potatoes with brown gravy and a big ladle of sweet green peas eased onto the edge of the potatoes (the peas were laid there on purpose, but they looked like they had been accidentally put on the plate).

Clarice personally delivered our food. I fell in love with mashed potatoes with brown gravy and green peas (my wife Barbara still fixes this meal for me), and I fell in love with Clarice. I would from that day on very affectionately, as best I could, wrap my arms around Clarice's massive legs (I could not reach her waist so I would hug her legs to greet her or say goodbye).

Sister Adrian later took me home to Mama and arranged for Mervin (my big brother) and me to start schooling at Holy Angels. I loved going to Holy Angels.

I would have many occasions to play with Jackie Sherrill and his little brother and eat in Clarice's kitchen. No meal Clarice ever prepared compared to the first she served us the day Jackie Sherrill and I became friends. I often wondered if I really had saved Jackie's life that day, or had Sister Adrian elevated my participation.

Time passed, several years went by and one morning I was in the cafeteria for breakfast. I looked around wanting to see Clarice and hug her legs but she was not there. Sister Adrian told me Clarice had left Holy Angels for a better paying head cooks job on Main Street in Biloxi. Sister Adrian told me that Clarice had three girls of her own and was happy to have more income. It had not occurred to me that Clarice had children of her own, or lived anywhere except at the cafeteria of Holy Angels.

I loved Clarice, and I believe she loved me (I believe she felt the love I had for her when I hugged her giant legs that were to me like the trunk of a "Giant Oak Tree Adorned With Spanish Moss). I, of course, could clearly see that Clarice was black, but I had no experience to comprehend how this could possibly be relevant. I never told Clarice that I loved her, but I did love her.

Years later, Jackie Sherrill would play football in school and college (he was one year ahead of me and was in some advanced honor classes with Barbara Miller, my future wife). Jackie was voted Mr. Biloxi High School and played football at Alabama on two national championship teams for legendary Coach Paul "Bear" Bryant. After graduation from Alabama, Jackie served as an Assistant Coach to Bear Bryant. Jackie was also Head Coach at The University of Pittsburgh, Texas A&M, as well as at Mississippi State, from where he would eventually retire.

Jackie Sherrill became a good sojourner spirit, a well-traveled man. I traveled the United States with Barbara

Miller Sonnier, and alone I sojourned to all parts of the world.

I remember reading a fair article about Jackie Sherrill in Sports Illustrated, SI "The Vault" December 24, 1990. "What Price Glory? Lusting for Football Success," by William F. Reed. Jackie Sherrill was hired by Mississippi State University after he resigned from Texas A&M in 1988.

(Many teachers labeled Cajun French speech as a low class and ignorant mode of speech, other Louisianans ridiculed the Cajuns as not being able to learn and be educated. As late as 1939, reports called the Cajuns "North America's last unassimilated white minority." Cajuns referred to themselves, even as late as World War II, as *"le francais,"* and all English speaking outsiders as *"les Americanes."*

The 1930's and 1940's witnessed the education and acculturation of Cajuns into the American mainstream. Other factors affecting the assimilation of the Cajuns were the improvement of transportation, the leveling effects of The Great Depression and the development of radio and motion pictures, which introduced young Cajuns to other cultures. Cajun culture survived and resurged. After World War II, Cajun culture boomed as soldiers returned home and danced to Cajun bands thereby renewing Cajun identity.)

The Sisters of Mercy and fine people like my Clarice helped the Sonnier and Louviere` families in our assimilation within the confines of Biloxi, Mississippi.

Yes, We Did Build That
"Oui, nous avons fait construire ce"

At one point in my young life we lived in a vacated shotgun style café; the rented café was one of our temporary homes. The building was located on the north side of Old Highway 90 (across the highway from Marvar's Factory on the south side of 90, at the corner of Myrtle Street, near the front beach, on the Gulf).

Our house was drafty and had no heat. The only air flow came from a huge window fan in a window off the east-side of the establishment. The building had an old food service bar that was about ten feet long. I found our new home interesting and quite comfortable, and I was content to live there.

Our entire family loved seafood, but often we could not afford it, even though my Mama and many other relatives worked in the seafood factories. My uncles, on the Louviere' side of the family, sometimes brought Mama seafood to prepare for our meals.

I remember on one such occasion that my Mama's eldest brother, Uncle Poncho as we called him, brought us a bag of oysters. When Mama returned home from working at the factory she shucked the oysters in preparation for our evening meal. Mama then prepared a batter (a familiar French recipe of yellow cornmeal, salt, pepper, and milk or egg) and fried some oysters in lard (naturally she used her black cast iron skillet).

(I might note that sometimes she dipped the seafood in the seasoned milk and egg liquid then dipped or rolled the items in the dry cornmeal, then fried. Other times, she made an actual batter of the milk, eggs, cornmeal, salt and pepper and dipped the seafood into the batter to coat, then fried. Yellow cornmeal makes a crunchy coating and it is delicious.)

66

On another occasion, my Uncle Cyrus (Bit) Louviere, Mama's youngest brother, brought us a bushel basket of crabs. I can still remember Mama removing the eggs from the female crabs (legal at that time), she left some eggs with the crabs, and then she put the remainder of the eggs in a pan to *sauté*. That was a meal to remember. The fragrance was overwhelming and the sauce, with the salty reddish eggs with the *sautéed* crabs (blue crabs), was delectable eaten over white rice. There were many good days as Mama and Daddy kept us warm and safe. I was content.

We lived close to the Louviere` family and spoke mostly French, with occasional broken English and Cajun French mixed in. Our neighbors were a mix of exotic cultures. We, Sonniers and Louviere`'s were of Louisiana, our minds and hearts said we were Biloxi Sojourners (Traveling Spirits).

While we lived on Myrtle Street my Mama and Daddy realized we needed more room for our family. We moved to a house on 1st Street a block from St. Michael's School. I recall living there when my sister Judy was born. We lived there until I was in the sixth grade. It was about this time, during my sixth grade school year, that my Daddy made a deal (a handshake contract with Mr. Higgins, his Foreman at Keesler Air Force Base). I was to eventually learn what deal my Daddy had made.

(Mervin and I, like so many other young Biloxi boys, had taken to wearing white cotton tee shirts and blue jeans. The style then was to fold your blue jeans high at the ankles. We often wore only Japanese thongs, flip flops as we called them, everywhere we walked. Most of us wore tennis shoes when we attended school.)

While struggling to make a decent living my Daddy continued his many years of service at Keesler Field. Daddy was a Civil Service Roofer/Carpenter. He was industrious, but had education limitations (reading, writing and arithmetic). Daddy was constantly telling us, "We are going to build our own house, you'll see."

One morning I could hear Daddy in the kitchen (my bedroom was next to the kitchen), and I walked in as he cooked his breakfast and prepared his lunch box. Daddy turned from the gas stove, looked down at me, and I was quite upset as he began talking about the dream he had just wakened from. With great emotion and tears streaming down his face, he said let's not wake the others.

Daddy sank into a chair at the kitchenette table and began relating an incident of incredible hurt that he experienced as a young barefoot Cajun boy. (My grandparents sharecropped farmland near Rayne, Louisiana.) Daddy began his account with the landowner's wife, Mrs. Broussard. Mrs. Broussard had sent her housemaid to my Mama, Olivia Sonnier, asking that I get her some fresh corn and other vegetables from the Broussard fields. I quickly brought her what she had asked for. Mrs. Broussard gave me a big tin bucket full of milk as a thank you. When her husband walked out of the big hay barn and saw the bucket of milk he got really mad. Mr. Broussard grabbed the bucket and yelled at his wife, "Don't give charity to those people, they will keep coming back for more. More of them will expect more and more charity, and they won't ever stop coming."

Mrs. Broussard tried to tell her husband about her request for vegetables, but Mr. Broussard said, "Those people get enough from the Broussard Farm every day working as sharecroppers. They think they are the ones who own my place and not me." Mr. Broussard kicked the milk bucket over wasting all that good milk that we needed back home.

Daddy said that Mr. Broussard told him, "Stay away from my wife." Mrs. Broussard told her husband that I was just a boy, just a baby. Mr. Broussard run me off that day, and I never went to that house no more me, no (Cajun dialect).

Papa m`a dit que M. Broussard lui dit: "rester a l`ecart de sa femme," et elle a dit qu`il etait juste un garcon, juste un bebe.

Il me faire sortir ce jour-la, et je ne suis jam ais a la maison ne m`a pas.

My Daddy was hurt badly by Mr. Broussard's stinging words of prejudice. Mr. Broussard was a Cajun, and that made his insults hurt even more. Mr. Broussard had become successful and greedy. My Daddy said to me, "That Mr. Broussard did not want no Cajuns around his family. No (Cajun dialect)." Mr. Broussard had shouted to me as I was leaving, "Stay away from my daughter and my wife." My Daddy told me something incredible, he said, "I forgive him me, yes" (Cajun dialect). *Mon papa m'a quelque chose d'incroyable: "Je lui pardonne-moi, oui."*

Daddy cleaned himself up, he was already tired, but he left for work at 4:00 a.m. We never spoke of the "Mrs. Broussard and the milk bucket" incident again.

My Daddy worked hard and made use of every skill he acquired while he learned English and lost his French language, but retained his rich Cajun accent. Mama and Daddy insisted that we speak only English, at all times, but especially while at school. It was against the law to speak a foreign language in American schools.

(Although the speaking of Cajun French has been crucial to the survival of Cajun traditions, it has also represented resistance to assimilation. Whereas, Cajuns in the oil fields spoke French to each other while they worked, and still do. Cajuns in public schools were forced to abandon French because the Compulsory Education Act of 1922, passed by the United States Government, banned the speaking of any language but English, at school and or on school grounds.)

The day to start our own house finally came. Daddy made a deal with Mr. Higgins to tear down and remove every piece of his abandoned dilapidated old family farm house located in Vancleave, Mississippi. Mr. Higgins told Daddy that he could have the materials for free if he removed the lumber from the farm property; he also told Daddy that he would provide his own old pickup truck and the gasoline for Daddy's use in the hauling.

We (Daddy and I) tore down the old house and moved all the lumber to the site of our future home on Oak Street. We saved all the nails so that we could straighten them later for reuse, and we saved thirty cinder blocks and both large three foot wide cement steps. My Daddy was very frugal, he had to be.

Daddy had purchased a small piece of marshy property at the corner of 8th and Oak Streets. The lot was close to our soon to be neighbors, Mr. and Mrs. Eli Flowers on the north, Son and Letty Illich on the east, Mr. and Mrs. Otis St`amant across from us on Oak, and Mrs. Joe Brush across from us on 8th Street, at the corner of 8th and Oak Street.

It was extremely hot on the days that we worked, but Daddy rarely stopped, and when he did he stopped for only a few minutes to drink cold water from the well behind Mr. Higgins old house. Daddy would take off his hat and wash his face and hands. On one of these breaks I could see that he had pine sap on his hands. His palms and fingers were bleeding from blisters. Daddy poured some kerosene on his hands and washed the kerosene off with a bar of soap; he then rinsed his hands over and over with the cold well water.

As we worked side by side, I never said a word about his hands, but listened as he told me to keep the Twenty Mule

Team Gloves on my hands. Later, when alone I cried as I thought of my Daddy's hands and how much they must hurt. Daddy made me take a lot more breaks than he did.

When we had finished working out in the country, we loaded the pickup to haul everything to our property on Oak Street (side by side, Daddy and I would clean up the Higgins property after each day's work). The loaded truck made numerous trips, day after hot day, from Vancleave to our property at the place known as "Across the Tracks" and "The Back Bay of Biloxi."

As we were stacking our bounty of wood, Daddy would say, "This is how your Grandpa Sonnier taught us to stack firewood for our home fires when I was young." "Put some wood down like this and then stack the others across like this," he explained. I listened and learned (when Barbara and I lived in Virginia, I used this technique to stack my firewood).

Daddy had already laid some 2x4's and 4x4's across the ground parallel to each other. We then laid all of our treasure (Daddy called the materials treasure) in neat piles across those boards. We used this process to keep the treasure from getting water logged and rotting. After we had carefully stacked the wood, we covered the stack with a large tarpaulin. Each time we completed a stack of treasure we would cover it and then tie each bundle with rope (protection from the weather and thieves). Mr. Higgins loaned Daddy the tarpaulins and the rope.

After we had finished removing our treasure from Mr. Higgins property, we talked about starting to prepare the wood and laying the cement squares for our cinder block bases to sit on. Daddy laid down some boxes and as a favor one of his friends poured cement for the house supports (this is when I learned about favors). These blocks would support the foundation cross beams to create a floor for our house. My Daddy seemed to grow larger in my eyes every day.

At the completion of each of our work days, Daddy would say what our work plan would be for the next day. Every morning he would talk about and repeat again and again our plans for the day. Daddy looked happier and happier after each day's tasks were completed. (The City of Biloxi, Harrison County, approved Daddy's plans and sketches and he was issued his builders permits.)

Daddy and I laid the cinder blocks on the cement bases and began building the floor of our house. Again and again, Daddy taught me the necessary skills I needed to help him build our new house. I learned to use a short and long crowbar, how to properly grip a hammer handle for maximum effect in pulling, driving and or straightening nails (he would say, we straighten these used nails to save money, we do not know how much we save, but we have savings). There are many tricks to using tools efficiently, and my Daddy knew them all.

During the time we were working on the house, Mama was either in a factory or taking care of my little sister Judy or my older brother Mervin. Mervin would help Mama and I would help my Dad. This was our family arrangement because for some reason Daddy and Mervin could not get along very well. Mervin also went with Mama to the factory and sometimes shucked oysters (he preferred this).

If we three children were left home alone to care for ourselves, because both Mama and Daddy worked, Mervin would fix our meals. One of my favorite meals that he prepared was left over rice tossed in a black skillet with some eggs, green onions, and bits of left over chopped ham. Mervin would add salt and pepper to taste, and voila, *et fini*, a masterpiece. The fragrance and taste was great, and I thought my Big Brother was swell.

Daddy and I built the walls and the frames for windows and raised each wall securing one to the other as we progressed. We then installed the ceiling beams and the roof in much the same way. Daddy would have different friends visit, and I would watch and listen as they provided him with helpful advice and freehand sketches on notebook paper (each sketch had dimensions and details, with step by step instructions).

An electrician friend came and did our wiring in exchange for Daddy's help with his roof and carpentry on the friend's house. After all of the integral wiring and plumbing were done, we finished the roof and started covering the exterior walls with boards (these boards were rough oak) that we specially mitered to fit into each other. We used a skill saw to make the mitered cuts until the saw burned up.

The skill saw burned up because the wood we cut was so hard. At this point, Daddy made a template and showed me how to use the template to mark the boards that I would cut using a hand saw. Hand sawing was not the way to make progress, and it was very difficult and slow for both of us. I knew it was agonizing for my Daddy, because I saw him slumped over as he sat on a cinder block crying, sobbing sounds, with his hands in his long curly black hair. Daddy would not look at me when he sat sobbing; he would pull out his handkerchief, blow his nose, and then after a short time he would stand, and I knew he was strong again and ready to begin working as he would say, "Let's get to work cowboy." I was nine or ten years of age at this time.

Mr. Higgins loaned Daddy a powerful electric saw. The electric saw was made by Black & Decker (The B&D Trim Saw was aluminum and was assembled together real solid and it was heavy) and could be adjusted by hand much easier, especially by me, to cut deeper or at angles. (Later in life I was to become the Senior Quality Engineer for Black & Decker, Power Tool Division in Tarboro, North Carolina.) Sojourner/Traveling/Assimilating.

As we sawed and placed board after board on the exterior walls of our house Daddy told me, "Cowboy, we have some friends coming to put in the electricity, the gas pipes, and the water pipes and meters." Days, weeks and months went by and men came as Daddy said they would. Daddy would tell me, "I'll help Mr. Toche or Mr. Lamey with such and such in exchange for what they are helping me with." They always came and he always helped them. Yes, we and they did build that.

I recall Daddy saying that with the way we were building our house, if a hurricane came it would have to roll the house to break its spine and pull apart the walls. He said that the hurricane waters would have to pick the house up off the cinder blocks and wash it out into the Gulf to destroy it.

Mervin started helping us when he was not working somewhere else, and he and Daddy seemed to get along just fine. My Daddy said more than once, "We really needed Mervin's help." When Mervin did come to help us everything would proceed much more smoothly, and Daddy seemed more resolved and sure that we could complete the house. Mervin always worked extra hard to satisfy himself, and I believe, to prove his worth.

After we had completed the outside walls of the house some friends placed light green shingles on the outer walls, as someone else worked on the roof. When the roof was finished we placed insulation in the rafters and started to put up sheetrock on the interior walls. We did not know what we were doing with the sheetrock, and Daddy had run out of friends to exchange favors with; also, Daddy was tired of working away from home for others. The sheetrock needed to be properly installed so Daddy said, "I'll go ask Annie (my Mama's oldest sister, she lived on 1st Street next to St. Michael's School) what to do." Aunt Annie Louviere` Hebert had prior experience building her own house, and she came to our rescue. Yes, she did build that.

Aunt Annie knew how to expertly install sheetrock. She instructed us that you had to use special galvanized nails to install the sheetrock to the support wood, then float, sand, apply primer to the sheetrock, and lastly you had to paint the sheetrock for finished interior walls. Aunt Annie was patient with us and taught us what we needed to know to finish our house.

More than once Aunt Annie said, "I can do anything I put my mind to, anything at all." Annie Hebert (pronounced, Hee Burt, and not Ay Bayer) had wavy gray hair which fell to her shoulders, she was very slender, but wiry and strong for her barely five foot two inch height. She was strong from years of hard work in the Louisiana sharecropper fields and in the Biloxi seafood factories. Aunt Annie was a no nonsense woman, but sweet as could be with all of her family (the Louviere's, Heberts, and Sonniers). It seemed to me that Aunt Annie could do anything! She was like "Giant Oak Trees Adorned With Spanish Moss." Aunt Annie raised two sons the eldest was Everett (Nago) and Tommy was the youngest.

Aunt Annie would help supervise Daddy's floating while Mervin and I sanded what Daddy had previously floated (Aunt Annie made us wear little face masks for protection from all the dust caused by the sanding). To a beginner the long process for finishing sheetrock to be painted (ceilings and walls) was overwhelming. Soon after we began painting, Aunt Annie told us we could finish the rest ourselves, and we did not need her help any longer. Mama and Daddy thanked her and offered any favors she would ever need, call us they said, and we all hugged as she left our house.

I would remember the significance of favor swapping and somehow I realized that this was foreshadowing events in my future. I understood this to be a plausible way of conducting business transactions while keeping the government taxation at bay and out of our business.

75

Daddy drove Aunt Annie back to her house that night. She would come occasionally to inspect our work, and one day she told us that we could move into the house and continue to work on finishing the inside. From that time on we saw less of Aunt Annie. Judy, my baby sister, would ask about her and where she was. "When is Aunt Annie coming home?" Judy would ask.

We now had a car, and after work Daddy would occasionally pick Aunt Annie up and bring her to our home (the home she helped build).

Our car was shiny black with a great deal of chrome finish. Daddy bought the car with money that he managed to save while building our house. Money saved because he and friends traded work favors. Having a car made our lives easier, especially Daddy's. He could now drive the car to work (he did not have to ride a bike). Our car was an older model 1948 Ford that had running boards on each side and a visor over the front windshield. Daddy said it was a collector's car; he said he was proud to own it.

As we worked every day to complete our home we would see and hear of family and neighbors building and completing their own houses (Daddy continued, when he could, to help friends and neighbors with favors, and I came to comprehend the significance attributed to this custom. I would learn and practice exchanging favors, in my line of work, the rest of my life.)

(I must emphasize again that after World War II, Cajun culture boomed as soldiers returned home and danced to Cajun bands thereby renewing Cajun identity. Cajuns rallied around their traditional music in the 1950's. In the 1960's this Cajun music gained attention and acceptance from mainstream America. On the whole, the 1950's and 1960's were wonderful times of further mainstreaming for the Cajuns.)

One year from the start date we completed our home. The year was 1954. I know that it was 1954 because that is when The Everly Brothers were very popular, and we first heard Elvis Presley on radio. We watched Elvis on television and in the movies. Everyone talked about how charismatic Elvis was. Elvis movies such as "Love Me Tender" and "King Creole" were very popular. We sang songs of the era that we heard and continued making progress in the finishing of our house/home.

I can vividly recall one particular night the television was playing in the living room. Daddy had already retired for the night, but he was still awake listening to goings on in Little Rock, Arkansas. All of the lights in our small home were off. There were the usual night silhouettes, shadows, and soft lights that the picture from our television cast upon our walls and floors. These silhouettes and shadows gave the interior of our house a settled peaceful ambiance.

I asked my Daddy about the Little Rock turmoil. I wanted to know why the black kids could not go to the better white schools. I asked my Daddy, "Why is it we are not letting the black kids go to the white schools? Why are there all white and all black schools anyway?" Daddy answered (in his Cajun dialect and rich accent) saying, "I don't know why that is, me, no, they pay taxes, yeah." My Dad's answer was an excellent and sensible answer to a complex question and problem. I knew then that my Daddy had common sense, and that he could, with the sensitivity of a person who had suffered discrimination himself, identify with all people in search of a more equal life, and their own ethnic and cultural assimilation.

I believe that Reverend John Isgood had the same kindly sentiments at the time of his lead from behind efforts in the wade-ins on Biloxi Beach. The difference was that many of the wade-in participants had criminal records and were agitators who would never return to Biloxi Beach after causing serious trouble for the local populace. Historically, it is true that there was very little participation in the wade-ins. The planned objective of the wade-ins was to affect the future of a geographic region of The United States of America.

That night passed slowly (Mama was working at Mary's Drive Inn helping to make some of the best po'boy sandwiches in Biloxi), and my Daddy and I worried about all the kids (black and white) and The Little Rock 9.

The very next day, we started work anew trying to finish our own little castle. Daddy saved money and would pay-as-he-went for other materials to continue improving our home. He purchased and installed kitchen and bathroom cabinets and eventually built a carport with a utility room for my Mama's GE washer and electric dryer. We, not some bank, owned our home. Also, our English was getting much better and our lives were improving.

I attended Biloxi High School and several years later in 1962-63 my family would begin moving from the house on Oak Street to a new home in Virginia City, a new development in North Biloxi.

The house at 802 Oak Street would withstand the assault of Hurricane Camille in 1969. Later, Hurricane Katrina would fail to wash our house into the Gulf of Mexico. Thanks to my giant oak tree gripping it firmly under its branches and holding the house next to its strong thick trunk. After Hurricane Katrina, the city and county would have to disassemble our house and haul it away. This was quite a tribute to our family teamwork and the strength of our "Giant Oak Trees Adorned With Spanish Moss." *"Geants chenes orne de mousse espagnole."*

(Historical fact is that Cajuns established settlements in the Louisiana-Texas border regions. Texans refer to the triangle of the Acadian colonies of Beaumont, Port Arthur, and Orange as Cajun Lapland because it is where the land of Louisiana and Texas lap over into each other.

South of the prairies and their waterways is the coastal wetlands. This is one of the most distinctive Cajun regions in North America. This region of Cajun settlement is central to their image. The culture and seafood cuisine of these Cajuns has represented Cajuns to the world. Cajuns have always been considered a marginal group, a minority culture. Language, culture, and kinship patterns have kept them separate, and they have maintained their sense of group identity despite difficulties. Cajun settlement patterns have isolated them and Cajun French has tended to keep its speakers out of the English speaking mainstream (these are documented historical facts).

Rene` and Mae
"reh nay"

Daddy's brother and sister, Uncle Rene` and Aunt Mae, learned from New Orleans and Baton Rouge, Louisiana newspapers that Louisiana residents, mostly Cajuns who had been sharecroppers in or around Jennings, Louisiana, could seek/apply for legal regress for land and or chemical rights and or financial settlement with various oil companies.

In other words our family could get money for having sharecropped on certain land in Louisiana. My Aunt and Uncle needed $300.00 from themselves and each of their other siblings to hire lawyers for their representation.

Daddy and Mama decided that this was too much money and too much of a risk. My parents thought it might take twenty or thirty years to settle. Only after all those years to learn that it was wasted money and effort.

My Uncle Rene` wrote a letter for my Daddy and his other siblings to sign giving him authority to represent all Sonnier siblings. He moved forward with slow deliberate progress for nearly twenty years. Finally, the oil people wanted to settle the claims instead of going to court.

Oil companies decided to settle with many of those who had been sharecroppers. On behalf of all his siblings, Uncle Rene` settled on a monetary amount per sibling. My Mama and Daddy were shocked when Uncle Rene` and Aunt Mae gave them the good news and a check.

The money was deposited into my Daddy's Biloxi bank account. My Mama is deceased and my Daddy lives in assisted living in Ocean Springs, Mississippi. His money, to my knowledge, is in joint checking and savings accounts with my Dad and my brother Mervin Joseph

Sonnier listed as account owners. My brother is my Dad's legal Fiduciary and Executor of his Last Will and Testament. Joe takes good care of our Daddy.

Son and Johnny Illich

Johnny Illich: My Mama's sister, my Aunt Menora Louviere`, married Johnny Illich. They lived in Biloxi on a street that was located near Mary's Drive Inn (Mary's was located on the corner of Lee and Division Streets; they sold great po'boys).

Aunt Menora and Uncle Johnny had three sons, Stanley (West Point Officer/Pharmacist), Alvin (a park ranger who was named after Alvin York, the most decorated soldier in WWI. Alvin York was from Tennessee and received The Congressional Medal of Honor for his WWI heroism.), Donald (Donnie) my Godson, and one daughter, Margaret (Margie).

Their house was just across the salt marsh from the back of Nichols High School's swimming pool (Nichols was a school for blacks, the only school in Biloxi with a pool, the pool purportedly was to keep the blacks off front beach). Just across from the Illich's there was more salt marsh and a swamp bridge. Across the swamp bridge, toward Biloxi Bay lived the Hamm family, the Simmons family (both families related), and down from them was The Dixie Café, Marguerite Teller Miller's (Barbara Miller Sonnier's paternal grandmother) establishment on Bayview Avenue.

My Uncle Johnny had served in World War II. He was wounded in action; a real life war hero. According to my Mama, Uncle Johnny had been wounded in the chest and head.

Uncle Johnny loved to go squirrel and deer hunting. Daddy and Uncle Johnny would go hunting whenever possible, and from time to time, my cousin Alvin and I would join them. I learned from Uncle Johnny that hunters can tell whoppers of stories.

While deer hunting near Wiggins, Mississippi, Uncle Johnny taught me some martial arts, and he told me about Alvin York from Tennessee. He also told me about Audie Murphy, an American soldier from Texas. He told me that Audie Murphy served in World War II and was that war's most decorated soldier (both he and Alvin York received distinguished medals from many countries). There were movies made of both Alvin York's ("Sergeant York") and Audie Murphy's ("To Hell and Back," was the movie about Mr. Murphy in which he played himself) lives and war experiences.

Uncle Johnny talked for quite some time about himself and then he cried, and we separated and walked into the woods, never to talk about war again. Our families hunted wild game together, raised and slaughtered hogs together, and told each other stories.

Uncle Johnny gave me some good advice, something which he had learned while serving in the Army. "Keep your mouth shut and listen," he said, "Do what you are told and never volunteer." Uncle Johnny continued, "When in combat get out of the open, hide behind trees, rocks, and walls." Also, he continued, "Be quiet, stay down, stay silent, listen and listen some more, be quiet, be quiet."

Uncle Johnny and his brother, Son Illich (our neighbor) were self-deprecating. They both laughed about themselves. They told military, fishing, hunting and especially family stories. These guys were Master Storytellers, and for their kindness and gentle ways I loved them both.

My Dad used to slaughter hogs for people (he traded his expertise for pork). He was an expert at this process. Daddy would slaughter hogs for Uncle Johnny and Son. When Daddy slaughtered a hog he would drive a bayonet between the hog's eyes into the hog's brain. Then he would grab the handle of the bayonet with his right hand

and reach around under the hog's throat with a sharp machete and slit the hog's throat from ear to ear (he performed these actions just like my Grandpa Sonnier had taught him). The first time I saw my Dad kill a hog in this fashion my knees buckled, and I went down on one knee. I would remember the machete and the slaughter the rest of my life.

On several occasions while hunting, Uncle Johnny and I would spot one another and visit quietly (so as not to disturb the wildlife). The woods near Wiggins were quiet and we did not use dogs. These visits were special to me. Uncle Johnny would take a few minutes to show me some judo and jujitsu moves, along with Korean holds, and a little French Martial Arts he had learned while in Boot Camp special training during the War.

One of my Uncle's best moves was a neck grab and hold from the rear. Another move was a swipe or kick with the foot to the side of an enemy's knee. Uncle Johnny refrained from talking about where he had served or what had happened at any place at any time except his Boot Camp.

Self-deprecation by my uncle was hilarious, he loved to laugh at his own jokes, and once when he had managed to stop laughing he said, "Your Daddy can't hunt, and he has no luck, but he sure can dress a deer and slaughter a hog better than any man I ever met." After he told me this, I was even more proud of my Dad. Uncle Johnny's stature increased in my eyes, because of his respect for his brother-in-law. I loved both my Uncle Johnny and Dad even more after that.

Son Illich: Uncle Johnny's brother, Son (Dago) Illich, was another character; he loved to tell a short story about his US Army days. Son Illich would tell any visitor to his home on 8th Street his version of his Boot Camp experience involving latrine digging.

According to Son, he and a couple of buddies from Biloxi dug the finest latrine ditches the US Army had ever seen. Son related that his Platoon Sergeant was so proud of him and his buddies that he had them permanently assigned to oversee latrine ditch digging, a status the Biloxians considered prestigious. My family lived next door to Son Illich and his fine family for many years, and during those years he would often tell his latrine story. I would patiently listen to him because he listened to me, a mere youngster, as though whatever I had to say was important to him.

I knew after hearing many of Johnny and Son Illich's stories that I wanted to tell stories just like my two heroes had told me. True they had not become pogie men (veterans coming back from a war with no place to go), because they returned to their homes and families. I believe, as with many men and women from small towns who serve/served in the military, serving their country was/is one of the high points in their lives, and Son Illich was a great example of this.

Son Illich was a gentle charismatic storyteller extraordinaire, because he belittled himself and then elevated his importance in the same breath. He would then laugh at his feigned ignorance that ditch digging was a very laudable undertaking (somebody had to do it he would say, why not me) which he loved doing in the performance of his military duty.

Many, so called adults, seemed to not take Son seriously, and act as though he was a little touched in the head. Son was touched all right. My friend, Son Illich, was touched by God with the ability to tell his Army story, just as my Grandpa Sylvester Louviere` (Papo) had told Mervin and I his story as we sat with him on his front porch.

(All veterans have a story to tell, they just need someone who wants to listen. Barbara and I enjoyed talking with her Daddy, Carl Simmons, about his World War II experiences. We knew, that he knew, that nobody wanted to share in his memories, we did.)

I listened to my Papo when he talked about the old pogie's, and I listened to Son Illich. I continue listening to our military men and women tell their war stories (be they touched in the head or not). I feel everyone should listen attentively, and always give our veterans respect.

I remember when yet another hurricane was about to strike Biloxi, Mississippi. Before this hurricane arrived our family, for safety, had moved into Howard #2 Elementary School located on Howard Avenue. When building our house, my Daddy had added extra cinder blocks under our floor beams adding height between our house floor and the ground. During the hurricane when the water rose under our house it reached the cross beams under the floors, but did not get into our house.

The hurricane left two feet of water in Son Illich's house on 8th Street. Son had some relatives from Baton Rouge and New Orleans, Louisiana come to help him with repairs to his house after the hurricane waters had receded. They ripped the sheetrock off of every wall, floor to ceiling, in order to let the structure dry out and air. My Daddy arrived too late to tell Son that all he had to do was drill three quarter inch holes just one inch from the floor, then cut the sheet rock with a roofers hook knife from both sides of the hole down to the floor allowing adequate drainage and drying. Mr. Higgins, my Daddy's boss at Keesler Air Force Base, advised my Daddy of this technique, but Daddy got to Son after the house was gutted. The technique that Mr. Higgins' told my Dad about would have meant less work and less expensive repairs for Son.

I would over a period of time learn that there are important life altering lessons you experience when assimilating with your own culture and neighbors of diverse cultures. I watched my family and others learn what changes to make in order to adapt to our environment; changes like drilling the holes in sheetrock to allow water to drain after a house has been underwater due to flooding from a hurricane; or when building a house in our area, add extra cinder blocks for protection from water. Help your neighbors. These actions are part of assimilation and adaptation of a culture.

Over the many years my Daddy and Son Illich would help one another and mutual friends and neighbors with favors. Many times I overheard my Daddy, Son, my Uncle Johnny Illich and other relatives and friends talking about helping each other. I most often heard men and women saying to my Daddy, "I owe you one, let me know if you need me, and I will be there for you Nole," and "You know you can count on me." Daddy always found he could count on them.

Son and or my Daddy would help our neighbors whether the favors were immediately returned or not. When times were hard and families destitute my Daddy would be there for them and they would return his favors. Most often families could fend for themselves, but not in the aftermath of hurricanes. Neighbors took care of one another or at least tried to; this was just simply understood as the proper thing to do.

After the hurricane and after Son had repaired his damaged house, he started working on his high school diploma. Son attended Biloxi Senior High School on Howard Avenue at night, two nights a week, three hours each night for almost two years before he graduated. He was proud! He had shown his children leadership and accomplished a remarkable task; considering he worked grueling jobs each and every day. My Mama, Daddy, my brother Joe, and all of our neighbors were amazed and proud of him.

Son knew his shortcomings and worked hard all of his life to steadily improve himself. One of Son's best skills, aside from being a master storyteller, was scraping and painting wooden houses for additional income. Son was a master painter and his services were highly sought after.

Son was like an uncle to me, and I relished his attention with storytelling. I especially remember his describing the smell of excrement as he worked preparing military latrines. Little did I know, but that his descriptive expertise would be a recollection in my mind that would help me to understand how scents draw animals to a food source. Son was a mentor and a leader that I learned to admire and follow.

As for Son, Letty, and their children Fredrick and Yvonne we would fish, cook, raise hogs, tell stories, and live together as neighbors for many good years. My Uncle Johnny Illich and his brother, Son Illich, were of small stature, but no two men could ever be bigger in my eyes.

Fire in Rayne

Our 1948 Ford would prove to be very useful to our family for many years. We traveled to Louisiana quite often for Christmas and or Easter holidays. Our entire family, consisting of my brother Mervin (Joe), my sister Judy Ann, my Mama, Daddy and myself, would travel to Rayne, Louisiana to visit my Dad's family. While in Rayne we not only visited Grandma and Grandpa Sonnier and an aunt in Crowley, but our Louviere` family in Jeanerette, Louisiana.

Occasionally, we visited with my Uncle Elfie, Daddy's brother, in Austin, Texas. Many of my Daddy's brothers and sisters lived in or near Rayne, and his family would gather in Rayne during the holidays for delicious French meals.

During our drive from Mississippi to Louisiana, Daddy always drove behind a Mack truck or some other large truck; Daddy had heard that it was safer to travel this way. We would start our trip very early in the morning. Our route was Highway 90 from Biloxi to Rayne. The trip was long and we usually arrived at Grandma and Grandpa Sonnier's around midnight.

Grandma Sonnier was always waiting up for us and would greet us in her broken English and Cajun French (I always understood what she said). We hugged and kissed all around our group and visited as Grandma started up her gas stove and prepared French Tarts (the pastry of these tarts was very similar to that of a Nabisco Fig Newton, but probably better).

As we talked, Grandma's hands moved rapidly as she formed the pastry dough into thin wedges similar to crepe suzettes. Grandma Sonnier placed her homemade fig preserves on each wedge and folded the pastry forming a beautiful tart. She then lightly floured the outside of each tart and began to carefully place tarts in her black iron

89

skillet (the skillet contained lard melted to the correct temperature for frying the tarts). The tarts emitted an unforgettable fragrance that filled the small kitchen as they sizzled around the edges.

As each batch of cooked tarts was ready, Grandma filled a plate and placed it in the middle of her table. She wanted us to eat the tarts while they were warm. There were jugs of milk on the table (fresh milk from their cow). We talked, ate tarts and drank the cold milk.

As I write about the fresh milk from my grandparent's own cow, I remember my Dad's story about Mr. Broussard kicking over the jug of cow's milk that his wife had given him as a thank you for bringing her fresh vegetables from the field. Daddy's family did not have a cow then, and they badly needed that jug of fresh milk. Mr. Broussard's cruelty from a Cajun Frenchman to a fellow Cajun Frenchman was tragic.

I thought that Grandma Sonnier was of Indian heritage because she had long black hair and wore it in a braid. Daddy told me that she was full-blooded French. I thought, without speaking, either way having some Indian blood in me would be all right.

The morning after our arrival at my Grandparent's house, the Sonnier family would begin to arrive. On one particular trip, I remember my Dad's brother and his family coming to visit, and their youngest son Jo`El played "Jambalaya" (a song that Hank Williams Sr. wrote) on his accordion. Jo`El played while the male adults went to the kitchen table to eat. The French custom was for the men to eat before the children and women (as a grownup I would question this custom).

While the adults were in the kitchen, we children were in the front of the house playing in front of a dark highly polished wood chifferobe (a handsome armoire style wardrobe and dresser for clothes; a free standing clothes closet). The chifferobe had some fake Easter basket grass lying in it. The older kids, older than me, had matches and coaxed me into lighting one of them. I did not know what a match was, and I was very gullible. The kids taught me how to strike the match and suggested that I toss it into the closet on top of the Easter grass. I lighted the match and tossed it into the chifferobe, and the Easter grass whooshed into a fireball, everyone scattered, but me.

The other kids (children) shouted, "Fire, fire, Ronnie started a fire." The other kids and co-conspirators were my brother Mervin, and first cousins Joann Hill and Steven Hulin. No one ever questioned or accused any of them. I alone took the rap. I was now known as a child arsonist.

The flames spread swiftly and the smoke billowed as the men closed the closet doors, and the women ran water into pots and tossed the water onto and into the closet. I heard fire trucks coming to our rescue as the flames grew larger and the smoke spread. All of us left the house and walked down the street to the safety of my Aunt Thelma Sonnier's house.

I felt closely watched each time we visited Rayne after The Fire in Rayne. I was looked upon as a child arsonist, and to my dismay no one exonerated me. Not my brother Mervin or my cousins. They would not accept any part in the event and it became the biggest stigma of my youth.

I was very young, vulnerable, and scared beyond belief, and I did not understand the bitter looks I was getting from everyone, except Grandma Sonnier. I was told to apologize to Grandma for starting the fire, I did. "Nothing to forgive, you are but a baby, it was our fault not yours. We should have watched over you more closely," Grandma said. "That is enough, say no more," Grandma said. *"C'est assez," N'en dites pas plus, grand-mere a dit."*

With Grandma's pronouncement, the fire fiasco ended and there was no more blame. Grandma extinguished the flames of accusation, and the smoke was clearing. Grandma Sonnier spoke the Cajun French language, her language was salty, her voice excited, her mood and words easy to translate. (My relatives never forgot that I was a child arsonist.) As the firefighters completed their work, Grandma told the entire clan to shut up, "Shut up, my babies are scared to death." Grandma said again, "Everyone shut up real fast." *"Tais-toi mes bebes sont morts de peur," dit grand-mere, et ils n'ont taire tres vite.*

Grandma's house was saved. Daddy and his brother, my Uncle Rene`, repaired it to almost mint condition (there was no smoke smell). I would have many nightmares of that dark and dismal day. The sounds of the wailing fire truck sirens and the pandemonium left me in a panic which I was unable to shirk. When I went to bed at night I was afraid. If I woke up during the night, I was too afraid to get out of my bed. I stayed in bed until daylight the next morning. I told no one of my fears; who was there to tell.

Darkness came over the rest of my young life, and I wet my bed every night until my teens. Finally, while in the seventh grade, Mervin told me one morning that I would never be able to have a girlfriend or get married because I wet the bed. Mervin said, "No girl wants to be wet on," he said. And so, I stopped.

Jo`El

Jo`El was my Uncle Boone's youngest son (Uncle Boone was Daddy's oldest brother), and destined to become well known worldwide, especially in country music. As a child Jo`El was a local hero because of his singing and accordion playing. At a very young age he reported news and weather on a local radio station, and as a teen he became known as The King of Cajun.

During his career Jo`El has had many crossover hits such as "No More One More Time" written by Troy Seals and Dave Kirby. In 1988 his accordion and costume were inducted into The Country Music Hall of Fame, and in 2009 he was inducted into The Louisiana Country Music Hall of Fame. These inductions were achieved due to his prowess as an instrumentalist, songwriter and singer.

Jo`El's rendition of "Louisiana," a song written by singer songwriter Randy Newman, is haunting. The spell-binding storytelling in the song, along with an accordion that talks, compels listeners to extreme emotion. Jo`El can feel and emit emotion with his physical presence and vocals. Having recorded and sang songs like these, it is no surprise that Jo`El is world famous.

"Louisiana"

"What has happened down here is the wind have changed

Clouds roll in from the north and it started to rain

Rained real hard and rained for a real long time

Six feet of water in the streets of Evangeline"

By: Randy Newman

On one visit to Rayne, Louisiana, I remember walking through Uncle Boone Sonnier's front door and on toward the kitchen at the back of the house. I recall the kitchen being setup just like our home in Sea Coast Camps, and Jo`El's Mama, Aunt (Yune) Eunice, and my Mama were in the kitchen seated at a kitchen table having coffee with Grandma Sonnier. The men, my Daddy, Uncle Boone, and Percy, Jo`El's elder brother, were in the living room.

Jo`El and I went out the back screen door, down the wooden steps and across a bare dirt backyard to a large wooden barn with a wooden corral fence attached. There were eight horses running around inside the enclosed area. The horses all came toward us to get attention from Jo`El. Jo`El grabbed an accordion off a bale of hay and started playing and singing.

While Jo`El sang "Jolie Blon" to the horses, cows, chickens and pigs, the animals seemed to be under a spell. They settled down as if in a trance and tried to get as close as possible to Jo`El and his sounds. Jo`El stopped his playing and singing, turned to me and said, "I sing to them, the animals, yeah, they are my babies (Jo`El spoke in a Cajun French dialect)." "They are my family, yeah!" Jo`El emphasized, "They love me."

(Because of the extreme popularity of the song, "Jolie Blon" and the historical message of the song, "Jolie Blon" is referred to as the "Cajun National Anthem." The first recording of the song "Jolie Blon," "Ma Est Partie" (Jolie) was made in 1928 by Amadie Breaux (born September 7, 1900), his brother Ophy Breaux and his sister Cleoma Breaux. The song was recorded on the Old-Timey Records label. The vinyl record is titled "Louisiana Cajun Music, Volume 5, The Early Years 1928-1938, (114)." This information is used for Historical and educational relevance.)

Jo`El finished his singing and cajoling the animals, and we stepped out of the barn into the all dirt yard. Jo`El walked up to the gate of the corral fence and swung the gate open releasing the eight horses. One particularly big horse (palomino stallion) ran up to Jo`El and reared up directly over him and made a pirouette (pirouette is technically a very challenging type turn, *pirouette a la seconde*, is where the dancer spins with the working leg in second position *a la hauteur*). The movement seemed graceful and impossible, but the horse accomplished the magnificent feat with ease and ran away around the small wooden house taking, what seemed to me, the lead of the other horses.

The speed of the palomino's running caused the other horses to run faster and faster, around and around the small house. The horses ran around the house as Jo`El began talking to them in his loud, childish, but rich Cajun French accent and dialect (mimicking his brother Percy in voice and style).

Suddenly Jo`El ran into the middle of the backyard in the path behind the eight horses and bent down on one knee, as in a prayerful position. The horses came back around the house and jumped over him. Jo`El immediately stood tall and ran behind them, a short distance, encouraging more speed while yelling yaaaagh, yaaaa. Jo`El would kneel each time he thought the horses were coming back around the house, and the horses would jump over him. (I believe that Jo`El was about ten years of age at this time.)

Jo`El's Mama yelled out the door, "Jo`El, leave those animals alone." Jo`El left the horses alone. The excitement was over. The ladies had talked themselves into an afternoon nap of probably one to two hours. Jo`El and I had to join the men in the living room while the ladies napped.

Jo`El deserved a chance to work in the music field, but with his Daddy as his Manager he was only nominally successful. After a while Jo`El returned to work as a farmer and lawn mower pusher until he met and married his first wife, Jamie. Jamie told Jo`El, "You can do better than this and play your music for a living." Jo`El's first wife loved him and encouraged his music.

Jo`El's Mama always told him, "You don't need that. No. You don't need that (just like my Mama)." Jo`El was determined, and with the help of Jamie, Jo`El Did Build That Music Business of His. Jo`El did need that.

Jo`El is a treasure to the Sonnier Family, Louisiana, and the world, we all love him. Barbara, my wife, and I attended a festival in Abilene, Texas where Jo`El was a featured performer (he was great). While living in Nashville, Tennessee, Barbara and I visited often with Jo`El and his wife, Bobbie. After one of his performances the four of us were talking near the grandstand, suddenly Jo`El said, "Ronnie, Barbara, you know my Mama has passed on, my Mama is gone, and he began to sob with deep emotion and mental anguish beyond my ability to describe. Jo`El and his Mama loved one another so greatly. I can only compare their love for one another to that of Elvis Presley and his mother. A love so deep and tender you would have to be in its presence to comprehend.

I believe Jo`El Sonnier is a Svengali and Impresario. Jo`El's acceptance and ascendancy is nothing short of a miracle. The miracle is a result of his God given talent, passion for hard work, success building and desire conversing with the sounds emanating from that box with keys vibrating with every stroke from his strong fingers.

Jo`El is a musical instrument in and of himself; he is a musical genius. Jo`El's music box/accordion is both a weapon and an instrument of wind sound. A small wind instrument, a descendant of or representative of the pipe organ placed in the hands of a small in stature maestro of wind sound.

Jo`El has evolved from a cute little Cajun boy to a real man. Cute no longer pertains to Jo`El or Cajuns. Jo`El is contributing, we are all contributing as entertainers, blue collar workers, white collar executives, educators, intellectuals, teachers, students, military, and yes we are Americans who continue assimilating into America's mainstream. We are functional and dysfunctional segments of American society, and it is our right to advance and choose the quality of our assimilation in every venue.

Cajun is not cute, Cajun is wonderful and grand, and Jo`El is a true American Svengali. "Cajun," n'est pas mignon, "Cajun," *est merveilleux, et grand, et Jo`El `est un vrai Americain Svengali.*

Giant Oak Trees Adorned With Spanish Moss
"Geants chenes orne de mousse espagnole"

I thought, like so many others before me, that "Giant Oak Trees Adorned With Spanish Moss" grew along Old Highway 90 because they had been planted in a row on either side. I was unaware that the highway was not as old as many of "The Giant Oak Trees Adorned With Spanish Moss," that grew along the beach for some twenty-six miles or so.

Much like the outer islands (Deer Island, Horn Island and Cat Island), the Giant Oaks and Live Oaks are a beautiful canopy, as well as a protective obstruction for the coast. The original coastal marsh lands have been replaced by seawall and sand beach. They serve as protection over and around Old Highway 90, Moss Point, Pascagoula, Biloxi, Gulfport, Handsboro, Waveland, Pass Christian, Mississippi City, and Bay St. Louis, Mississippi.

In amazement at the wonder of it, I remember thinking "what a tunnel" as I passed under those massive low hanging long limbs (branch tentacles hanging low as well as reaching high upward, ever so high into the sky even as the massive roots reached down deep into the rich earth and or across its surface, making it difficult for even tenacious St. Augustine Grass to grow).

The Giant Oaks thrived and protected, and continue to protect, the shores along the Gulf Coast. The Oaks also protect the many houses (people's homes) and businesses on the peninsula known as The Home of The Biloxi Indians.

This is the same Biloxi that is the place written about in "Biloxi Blues," the Neil Simon Play created into a 1988

98

comedy film of the same name, directed by Mike Nichols, starring a very young Matthew Broderick. The story is about young male recruits in boot camp.

I lived in the land which had been inhabited by the original Biloxi Indians. There existed a certain amount of comfort as I played and grew up under the protection of those massive sheltering Oak branches that sometimes hung so low they seemed to caress the very earth the roots grew from.

My family home on Oak Street, in Biloxi, had a Giant Oak in the yard. Our Oak was not as large as the Oaks adorning Old Highway 90, but it looked quite enormous to me as I stood under its branches or climbed or hung like Tarzan's son, Boy, from its branches.

Our Oak seemed to touch the sky and I would often climb it reaching ever higher, branch to branch. I would sit speaking to it and even caressing it like a friend. I would look out and over the roof of my house and those of my neighbor's houses while watching and waiting for the Oak & Division city bus to pass in front of our home.

I would think to myself, that is the Otis St`amant's house across the street. The St`amants (another Cajun French family) had lived only a couple of blocks from where I had seen the gator that ate Gumbo and met Lois Hebert earlier in my life.

As Mervin, Judy and I grew into teenagers we would continue to tune our radio into "The Whistler" and or the "Creaking Door.' Mervin and I were terrified when the whistling or creaking sounds interrupted the quietness of our bedroom, but we always looked forward to listening to our radio programs.

As we squealed from fear, and panic we were in fact delighted with the excitement it generated. Daddy would say, "You boys had better shut up and don't make me come in there." *Mon papa disait: "Vous feriez mieux de garçon enfermé .. et ne me faites pas venir là."* Daddy's admonishments would cause us to crave his attention, and we would scream until Daddy told us to turn the radio off. We appreciated that order because we were on the verge of wetting our bed.

We would listen to those radio mysteries into our teen years, and Daddy would always have the same reaction. Daddy tried to get us to settle down early because he awoke at 3:00 a.m., Monday through Friday, to go to his job at Keesler Air Force Base. Daddy adhered to this schedule for thirty years until he retired at age 50 due to my Mother's ill health.

We resided at 802 Oak Street as I grew into my teenage years. I completed the sixth grade at St. Michael's, went on to Biloxi Junior High School (referred to by students as Central Junior High School) and then to Biloxi Senior High, maturing with Barbara, until I left for the US Army in 1962.

It was while I attended sixth grade, taught by Sister Mary Joseph, that we built our home on Oak Street. We built the house with exterior walls of Oak wood. The house was constructed near and even under our Giant Oak.

Sister Mary Joseph had me memorize a prayer which she titled "A Soldiers Prayer." Sister Mary Joseph said this prayer was credited to Joyce Kilmer, a journalist who died on the front lines in France during World War I. With the reading and understanding of this poem, actually entitled "Prayer of a Soldier in France," I decided I loved poetry.

"Prayer of A Soldier in France"

My shoulders ache beneath my pack
(Lie easier, Cross, upon His back).

I march with feet that burn and smart
(Tread, Holy Feet, upon my heart).

Men shout at me who may not speak
(They scourged Thy back and smote Thy cheek).

I may not lift a hand to clear
My eyes of salty drops that sear.

(Then shall my fickle soul forget
Thy Agony of Bloody Sweat?)

My rifle hand is stiff and numb
(From Thy pierced palm red rivers come).

Lord, Thou didst suffer more for me
Than all the hosts of land and sea.

So let me render back again
This millionth of Thy gift. Amen.

By: Joyce Kilmer (1886-1918)

Prayers for Warriors: Psalms 44 and 54, King James Version of the Bible

During one particular school week, Sister Mary Joseph assigned our class the task of memorizing and reciting this poem in class. Friday, the day to recite our poem came and each student recited with hesitation, stutters and forgetting some lines. Classmates and Sister Joseph helped each student to completion.

I remember, I had not studied or learned a single line of the poem and was a little embarrassed at the thought of having to recite the poem. Sister Joseph started on the row to her left having each student stand to recite the prayer. I began reading a copy of the poem while listening to the other students. As my fellow classmates stuttered and stammered, their failures gave me the

101

courage to keep memorizing. I felt I could do just as well as they were doing when I recited before the class. I knew I could memorize enough of the poem to get help from Sister Joseph.

There were five rows with ten students on each row. The middle row was almost finished reciting, this left my dear friend Ray Broussard, Jenny Hightower and me to recite. I was listening, reading and memorizing faster than at any time in my young life. I did not want to disappoint Sister Joseph, myself nor have my classmates giggle at my failures.

Sister Joseph suddenly saved me by reversing the order of recital and beginning again with the front of the row on her right. "Time, I thought, I have more time," and I doubled down memorizing." I was over half way through the poem and gaining courage as others faltered. I pushed on not looking up, but listening to every prayer and wanting to know the prayer more and more. I enjoyed the magnificence and the true significance of the words.

It seemed only a few moments after the first recital that I heard Ray finish the poem. I was still memorizing when I heard Sister Joseph ask, "Are you ready Jenny Hightower?" Jenny recited her lines to completion with coaxing help from Sister. It was my turn. I began slowly and deliberately without mistake, although my classmates took my slightest hesitation as needing their whispers of coaxing words. I was brilliant and Sister Joseph knew it, everyone knew it, including myself. Everyone sat in stunned silence awed by my magnificence.

Everyone in the class laughed nervously. Jenny Hightower told me that she had not learned the poem and appreciated that Sister Joseph asked her to recite last. I knew at that moment, I could learn anything I put my mind to. Sister Joseph knew this and I sensed her new found respect for me. Sister Joseph knew I could do it, my broken French and English accent notwithstanding. Sister Joseph knew I could be a good student.

I was proud and began reading my first book checked out of the public library (The Old Biloxi Library which was built in Alamo style architecture). The first book I read was "Ivanhoe" by Sir Walter Scott, published in 1819.
On my own initiative, I memorized the poem "Trees," which was also eventually credited, by major experts to World War I front line journalist, Joyce Kilmer. Mr. Kilmer was assigned to The Fighting 69th. Joyce Kilmer was killed in action in France.

After I had memorized "Trees," I often perched in my tree, and while I gently stroked a branch, I recited the poem. As I recited "Trees," my "Giant Oak Tree Adorned With Spanish Moss" and I rode the very warm cross breezes from The Gulf of Mexico and The Bay of Biloxi.

"Trees"

I think that I shall never see
A poem lovely as a tree.

A tree whose hungry mouth is prest
Against the sweet earths flowing breast;

A tree that looks at God all day,
And lifts her leafy arms to pray;

A tree that may in summer wear
A nest of robins in her hair;

Upon whose buxom snow has lain;
Who immediately lives with rain.

Poems are made by fools like me,
But only God can make a tree.

By: Joyce Kilmer, 1886 – 1918

I remember the St`amants lived in Grego's Camp in a two story complex. There were many steps and porches in front of each family living space. This housing camp, on Old Highway 90, near Holy Angels Nursery, was a well-built wooden structure with a low maintenance shingle exterior.

All the seafood factory workers were poor French, Irish, Italian, German, English, Spanish, Polish, Greek, Yugoslavians (they were called Austrians), and many other ethnic cultures, etcetera et al; they all lived in Sea Coast Camps (at one time or another). The ethnic groups kept to themselves, after a while, they began to make friends with each other and assimilate (assimilate within and among the different groups and within the City of Biloxi). The Otis St`amant's were our neighbors on Pointe Cadet and on Oak Street. Otis, their son, was our neighbor, classmate and one of our best friends for life.

The Peninsula of Biloxi was extended and vastly improved by filling in the salt marshes with refuse. The trash was covered with topsoil (rich black dirt), one load at a time, by the citizens of Biloxi with help from the city and county.

Fisher people and shipbuilders improved Biloxi, one area of unimproved land at a time. The improved land was then rendered legally useable, saleable and taxable. Just as my family built their home at 802 Oak Street, my future father-in-law, Carl Simmons and his eldest daughter, my future wife, Barbara Ann Miller were taking a pre-existing small remodeled house and adding two bedrooms at the rear. The addition that Carl was building vastly improved the house at 1117 Bowen Street.

Carl also built a separate one car garage with a wash shed (utility room) at the back. He built his girls a playhouse (Barbara told me that she and her sisters considered themselves extremely lucky to have a place for their toys; a place to play safely). The playhouse was 8x8 feet square and 8 feet high. The structure had an open rafter ceiling, a grownup sized door and small windows on two sides for ventilation.

Violent storms and Hurricanes would come and wreak devastation, repairs would be made, and life would begin anew. We knew then that more hurricanes would come with their strong winds and high waters wreaking havoc, bringing destruction once more. A common cycle for the Gulf Coast of the United States and the residents therein.

Over time, strong hurricanes like Hurricane Camille (1969) would bring in tidal waves that would put many houses under water and cause severe damage along the Gulf Coast. During Camille's devastation, Barbara and I along with our four young children stayed in our home at 1104 Orleans Drive in North Biloxi. Years later, Hurricane Katrina (2005) then Hurricane Isaac (2012) would ravage Mississippi and Louisiana. These storms took their separate turns demolishing the Biloxi Peninsula and homes that we had built with our own hands.

Coastal residents knew that someday there would be a Hurricane Camille devastating our peninsula, damaging homes and businesses for miles. We knew that 802 Oak, the home that Dalton Sonnier and his sons Mervin and Ron built, and 1117 Bowen Street, the home that Carl Simmons and his oldest daughter Barbara Ann, remodeled, might not survive these destructive forces of wind and high waters, but did survive requiring much repair.

Many years after Camille (with her 200 mph winds and gusts) would come Hurricane Katrina (Katrina had up to and over 200 mph wind gusts) with winds that caused a thirty-four foot high wall of water to hammer and encircle the entire peninsula (Gulf and Bay waters merged over the Biloxi peninsula). The accompanying undertow (similar to a tsunami) placed the area under a deluge of water and when the water receded much of Biloxi was washed away, total destruction.

When Hurricane Katrina hit the Gulf Coast, it did in fact, destroy Biloxi washing most of it into the Gulf. Katrina destroyed homes and businesses that had existed for a long time, but we still remembered them, and "Yes, We Did Build Those Houses!"

Hurricanes seem to be accompanied by a dark sinister presence leaving everyone in their path (the hurricane's path) praying for an opposing good presence for protection before, during, and after the tragedy. Though distant observers when Katrina hit the Coast, Barbara and I, were none the less, horrified at the deaths and wide spread devastation of the Alabama, Mississippi and Louisiana Coasts.

During Katrina, my Daddy was living in a nice small trailer on my sister Judy Sonnier Domonousky's property in North Biloxi (his home suffered no damage, neither did my sister's house). My brother Mervin (Joe) Sonnier's home suffered roof damage, which in turn caused him more damage. The Sonnier family had been spared major tragedy. We learned that none of Barbara's siblings (Simmons) had sustained damage. Carl's widow, Ida Mae Hebert Simmons, had lost everything, was injured, taken to Louisiana and stayed in the hospital for several weeks. Ida was severely traumatized.

After Katrina, I traveled from our home in Columbia, South Carolina to Biloxi to check on my Father. After I arrived in Biloxi, my Daddy and I took a ride around Biloxi (this was several weeks after the Hurricane had hit, and the roads and Old Highway 90 were open to through traffic). I drove to the sites of mine and Barbara's previous homes in North Biloxi and Gautier (the houses were still standing), but I am sure that they had water in them during the onslaught of Katrina.

I drove my Dad to the site of our old home (that we built) on the corner of Oak and 8th Streets. The house was gone, not because Katrina had the power to take her, but because she had suffered such severe damage and had to be destroyed by the city. As my Daddy and I approached the corner where our house had stood, we could see standing majestically, its great trunk curling out of the earth, "Our Giant Oak Tree Adorned With Spanish Moss."

The Oak's branches were sparse, but they extended up and the tree seemed satisfied that it had done its job well. When the hurricane waters raged, the waters picked our house up off its cinder blocks and attempted to wash it into the depths of the Gulf's waters. My Daddy described to me how our old home had been found wedged under the branches of the Giant Oak tree in our side front yard.

I parked my car, left Daddy sitting inside, and walked to my tree. I walked across 8th Street, through the small vacant yard, unhindered toward my tree. I felt a kindred spirit, like a low electrical charge of adrenalin running through my body as I approached the Oak and touched one of the branches, and then stepped up, and onto curling roots at the base of the trunk.

Instantly there was quiet in the entire area, no breeze or movement of Oak leaves, as I continued touching her. I stepped up onto the base of the Oak, and we both knew the importance of our friendship, and I could feel her elation that I was home to share in her triumph over Katrina.

I recited Joyce Kilmer's "Trees" once again to My Oak Tree, and I felt a bond with her again. The stirrings of our past, and our new beginning, at that moment evoked a proud and knowing spiritual kinship that I could only remember experiencing one other time in my life. I thought back to another moment in time, on the safety and brotherhood I knew as I lay under the weight of the bodies of Snicker and Nickel in that monstrous warehouse in Vietnam.

My Oak Tree and I were reminiscing as my Daddy waited patiently watching our celebration from my car. Daddy left the car and with the aid of his wooden cane walked across 8th Street following the same path I had and joined in the celebration of our tree's majesty and victory over Katrina.

What did you say to that tree?" my Daddy asked. I told her, "Thank you." Daddy smiled. "Our house was wedged right here under her big branch and held by the Oak limbs. Only the crown on the rooftop of the house was crushed," Daddy said. Our house withstood the high winds, but was gutted by the water that was fifteen feet over the roof. When the tidal wave receded it washed through the house leaving it and the Oak tree holding onto each other.

Daddy said, "They had to break her (our house) rough lumber (oak) away from the frame and run over her with bulldozers and a crane. The workers then placed her piece by piece on big trucks to be hauled to front beach where there were piles of other houses and buildings waiting to be picked up and transported to landfills." Land on the peninsula was cleared so that someday new homes and businesses could be built. Yes, Biloxi residents did build that, yes, they did rebuild.

There were no other trees or houses for blocks around, only scrub bushes and remnants of smaller bushes with bare branches. Some trees had a mattress or toilet lodged in them awaiting the cleanup yet to be completed. When we had stood there, by the Oak Tree, we looked all around us and came to a realization that all of our neighbor's homes had been destroyed, but the neighbors were living safely elsewhere. Yes, they did build those homes.

Daddy and I drove north on Oak Street toward The Back Bay of Biloxi, and then turned right and drove along the Bay. We witnessed empty property where the Gollotts and the Weems had lived. As we drove, we saw remnants of factories already beginning their resurrection to seafood enterprise, buying and selling from fisher boats run by the tough fisher people of The Mississippi Gulf Coast.

We drove to where Barbara's family home had stood on Bowen Street, we saw another empty lot, and then we turned and drove back to Oak Street. Daddy and I drove south on Oak, passed Division Street traveling toward Old Highway 90. After crossing the railroad tracks just south of Division, we took a left where the metal salvage yard had been and drove toward where Joan Tiblier and her family had once lived. (Joan had long since moved to Ocean Springs where she had worked in education administration.)

Many of the old families rich in their diverse histories settled in the welcoming arms of the Mississippi Gulf Coast (the assimilation that they began continued). Vietnamese peoples joined these ranks and had moved into these areas replacing many of the French, Cajun, Irish, Slav's, English, Italians, Polish, Greek, German, Swiss, Spanish, Portuguese, African, Swedish, Norwegians, Chinese, Japanese, and Koreans on Pointe Cadet and near the Back Bay. All the previous residents had moved to other parts of Biloxi (north of the Back Bay), other cities, and other states as assimilation, progress and migration of the cultures continued.

There stood at the end of the Biloxi Peninsula a huge white structure, it looked undamaged; it was a Casino. Casinos and parking garages were standing tall at Myrtle

Street and Old Highway 90 and were undergoing repairs in order to reopen in a few months. Biloxi business and its versatile citizenry would rise again much like a Phoenix rising.

My Daddy and I traveled (sojourned) west toward Gulfport on Old Highway 90 toward the cemeteries (on the north side of Old 90) and found that gravesites had not been washed away. Further down Old 90, we arrived at my Mama's resting place in a cemetery mausoleum (near Beauvoir, Jefferson Davis' historical home and The Tomb of The Unknown Confederate Soldier).

Daddy and I found that there had been massive destruction in the cemeteries, and Mama's mausoleum had been damaged. The cleanup and repairs would take some time, and this was most disheartening to witness and know that my Mama's final resting place on this earth had been ravaged by Hurricane Katrina. My family took solace in the knowledge that Mama's spiritual body was with our God in Paradise, not in some hole in the ground or mausoleum. According to the media and coroner's office, many coffins had been washed out of their secured cubicles into the Gulf, but had returned to the beach, none were lost.

My Mama had won out against Katrina and my family was relieved, and we thanked God. My Mama had always been traumatized by the announcement of an approaching hurricane; she did not have to worry about Katrina.

There are those individuals who will never leave Biloxi, and I understand their feeling secure and happy there. Barbara and I moved on with our children improving our lives while living in numerous homes in other countries such as Germany and states such as Georgia, North Carolina, Illinois, Texas, Tennessee, Florida, Virginia, and South Carolina. We sometimes look back at Biloxi with both pleasant and unpleasant memories. As we were leaving Biloxi in 1978, much like Mac Davis' song, "Lubbock in My Rearview Mirror," we put Biloxi behind us as we moved forward with our lives (assimilating).

In our youth, Barbara and I along with our four children, appreciated small parks, the safe front beach, and the restaurants (with their fine seafood cuisine and ambience), but the ever increasing syndicate criminal element, and accompanying crime wave on this peninsula provoked us into moving away.

After three years in the US Army, we returned to Biloxi (from Germany via Columbus, Georgia) and rented a World War II era house on Kuhn Street (in the middle of the regional area where we both grew up). A short time later we purchased our first home at 1104 Orleans Drive in Cedar Grove, North Biloxi.

After eight years, we bought a second home in Gautier, Mississippi to be closer to Gulf Coast Community College where I studied and earned my Associates Degree in Quality Control Technologies. Gautier also put me closer to where I was employed, Litton Industries (Ingalls Nuclear Shipbuilding, Pascagoula, Mississippi). After receiving my Bachelor of Science Degree in Education from The University of Southern Mississippi, we decided to seek work away from the Coast. Our first sojourn, as a family took us to Tupelo, Mississippi.

Barbara and I never, over the years, considered the term dysfunctional family, but, it certainly describes our combined families, then and today. We try our best to not think ill of the Old Biloxi where we grew up feeling safe and happy. The quaint fisher town where there were neighborhood grocery stores and families lived in close proximity. Our Biloxi had "Giant Oaks Trees Adorned With Spanish Moss." *Geants chenes orne de mousse espagnole.*

Biloxi was a quaint fisherman's village that metamorphosed into a gambling utopia. A different Biloxi exists today, replete with Casinos, a literal heaven for tourists with money to spare or not. There exists a virtual crime wave creating revenue from gambling and taxes from gambling, while at the same time creating jobs in Casinos. This crime wave causes devastating carnage among the local poor. These captive poor frequent and seek escape, and or a short trip to wealth, like playing to win the lotto.

Biloxi may be a nice place to visit, but I would not want to live there again. The little fisher village with great restaurants and small cafes with ambience, small town atmosphere and people serving delicious seafood cuisine accompanied by the familiar accents of differing languages and wonderful cultures, is no more. That Biloxi has metamorphosed into something new and agreeable to current citizenry and tourists.

Carl Kemper Simmons Loved Children
"Les enfants ont adore Carl Kemper Simmons"

Sally Ann Goff Miller Simmons, Barbara's mother, had been a teenager when she met and married R. L. Miller. Sally was a beautiful young woman standing five foot seven inches in height. Sally had long wavy brown black hair, an olive complexion and deep brown eyes. Sally had a short waistline, small waist, long legs with slender ankles, and Miss Sally (as I called her) loved to dance. Most often Sally was very friendly with everyone, except Barbara.

A couple of years after R. L.'s death when Barbara was a toddler, Sally married Carl Kemper Simmons. During World War II, Carl served in the US Navy on the USS Curtis. The Curtis was hit with a huge multi-ton projectile (bomb), the bomb did not explode. The Curtis also had many Japanese Kamikaze plane attacks, but the Curtis was not destroyed, and Carl Simmons came back home to Biloxi.

Carl was, to my knowledge, of English and French descent. He was five foot eleven inches in height, had a ruddy light olive complexion and wavy brown black hair with a slightly receding hairline. Carl possessed a very sociable demeanor (he was a wonderful father to all his children).

Carl liked working, talking with and hanging out with fisher people, common people. Carl very occasionally, when his children were young, enjoyed beer and card playing at Black's Bar (a popular local tavern, beer joint) on Pointe Cadet. In spite of this rough social habit, Carl was firstly and foremost, a wonderful person with a strong good character and wonderful personality.

Over the years Carl would move on successfully to many forms of work. Carl worked on seafood boats, constructed wooden boats, made fish nets, was an oil field worker and Pusher, worked on an oil exploratory boat, and finally was an employee of Litton Industries (Ingalls Shipbuilding West Bank, Pascagoula, Mississippi); then he retired. I can still remember Carl making his own casting nets and taking them to the front beach to cast for mullet.

Carl's work involved considerable time traveling (Biloxi Sojourn Esprit) the oceans as a mate on a world class Marine Explorer vessel. While working on the explorer vessel Carl would live on many exotic islands and frequent local bars.

Carl loved Barbara Ann Miller (Simmons) and she loved him. Carl took it upon himself to care for and love Barbara in place of R. L. Miller. Carl's daughter Barbara was always a high spirited, lovely, affectionate, and caring girl. Barbara was a very smart honor roll student (she told me it made her so proud to tell her Daddy about her grades; he never failed to praise her, display that he was proud of her, and encourage her to continue doing well).

Most of Barbara's young life was spent sleeping back to back with her Maw maw Goff (I regret that I never got to meet Barbara's Maw maw; she died shortly before we met), or on a hide-a-bed couch in their family living room. Carl, when financially feasible, would make improvements to his modest home and Barbara would have her own bedroom.

Barbara metamorphosed into a beautiful five foot six inch raven haired teenager. Barbara was blessed with a lovely olive complexion, slightly round face, pretty nose, and rosy lips and cheeks. She had a small waist (short waist), long stocky legs, and over the years she would develop broad Esther Williams' swimmers shoulders.

Carl loved Barbara and raised her as his natural daughter along with his and Sally's other four children. Sad but true, the other children and Sally would not love Barbara as much as Carl did. The actions of the other children (her siblings) have haunted Barbara her entire life. As a young girl, Barbara participated in raising and caring for her siblings.

Barbara and I met in Junior High School, prior to that I had attended St. Michael's School, while Barbara attended Dukate Elementary (public school). Barbara had started attending Central Junior High School a year before me (I was held back a year, the nuns felt that I was immature).

When Barbara was about twelve and I was thirteen, my Mama had visited a hair salon across from the Buck Theater in downtown Biloxi. Mama came home excited and told me that she had seen Sally and her daughter Barbara at the hair salon. "You remember Barbara don't you?" Mama asked. "You played together when you were babies," she continued.

I did not remember playing with Barbara at all, and it is hard to understand, but I sensed somehow that I did know Barbara from somewhere, from some other time that I could not place. Barbara and I were destined to meet, date for three and a half years then marry on April 16, 1962.

(Cajuns usually marry among themselves and as a group they do not have many surnames; however, the original population of Acadian exiles in Louisiana has grown, especially by incorporating other people into their group. Colonists of Spanish, German, and Italian origins, as well as Americans of English, Scotch, and Irish origin became thoroughly acculturated and today claim Acadian descent.)

Barbara has recounted that her Daddy made an outstanding potato stew; a stew unadulterated by beef. The others, (as I call Barbara's siblings) also loved the stew and they would all beg their Daddy to fix some for a special meal when he was home from working in the oilfields (unfortunately this was before my time with Barbara, and I did not get to eat Carl's stew).

Carl could make a wonderful filet okra gumbo with seafood, chicken, and sausage and have it hot and available to visiting family and friends on holidays. Barbara told me that when she was young, they would have visitors on Christmas Eve into the early morning of Christmas Day. Their kitchen bar and table were full of baked ham, potato salad, pies and cakes. Carl usually kept a well-stocked bar also. (These are the things that many families in Biloxi did when Barbara and I were young.)

From time to time with the moon just right, Carl would gather his net or gig and lantern, and he and Barbara would take off to the front beach for a night casting for mullet or gigging flounders. Barbara, his side kick, would tag along to be his bag girl, and they would have a great time. After the catch was brought home, Barbara would be right there pitching in helping her Daddy with scaling and or filleting the fish. She told me they laughed and talked as they worked.

Carl would shuck oysters behind their wash shed, Barbara would not help with this, but as her Dad ate a large oyster from the shell, she would ask for a small one when he came across it. These rituals were ones that Carl and his daughter enjoyed, just the two of them alone, as they talked and laughed, and talked and laughed some more.

Carl, Barbara, Ida Mae Hebert Simmons (Carl's last wife), and myself would place nets out along both sides of the Old Biloxi Oceans Springs Bridge. We would all have a great time laughing, cutting up and possibly eating an ice cream from the local ice cream truck (Barbara got a kick out of buying her Daddy a treat; Carl enjoyed this also).

On one occasion as we were crabbing, I almost lost a crab trying to put it in a basket. The crab fell onto the bridge surface and scampered toward the side of the bridge (an opening for freedom from the crab boil pot). I threw my right foot out to stop the escaping crab only to find out this was a big mistake (I was wearing open toe flip flops). My foot was on the crab's back and the crab reached around and back, pinching my big toe with his big claw, tearing open the flesh of my toe. My toe was bleeding, and I was suffering severe pain and humiliation.

I screamed and tried to shake the crab loose, the crab hung on. Carl almost burst his gut laughing, at my expense I might add. We all laughed, it was fun even if I was suffering. Carl almost fell out of his lawn chair; we all laughed even harder. Carl had a great laugh.

Thibodeaux, Jordan, and Haas

I knew at the end of seventh grade that I had failed math. After school as I walked home, with my report card, I prayed earnestly to God to straighten it out in order that I might advance to the eighth grade in spite of my grade. I finished my prayer having made no deal except to try harder, and immediately thereafter I left my fate with and in God's capable hands.

Summer passed and school started again. I discovered that I had been placed in an eighth grade math class that was to be taught by a new teacher, Mr. Thibodeaux. A girl from the office came to Mr. Thibodeaux's class and announced, without preamble, that she was there for Ronnie Sonnier. The girl read from a cue card, "Ronnie Sonnier failed seventh grade math last year and must come to the office immediately, and from the office to be escorted to a seventh grade math class (this tactic seemed like the warden and the executioners of the prison were bringing me to the electric chair). At this point, I remembered that I had failed seventh grade math.

Mr. Thibodeaux would have none of that. He dismissed the girl who remained standing in the classroom by turning away from her, and he addressed me directly, asking, "Mr. Sonnier, do you promise to do your best in my class?' "Yes, I will do my very best," I promised.

Mr. Thibodeaux told the girl to return to the office and tell them that I was in his class and was staying in his class. "Tell the office that I will take care of Mr. Sonnier (sawn Yeah)," he said. Mr. Thibodeaux, with God's influence, saved me from total embarrassment and utter humiliation of failure (after all I had already repeated second grade while attending St. Michael's School).

As I reflect back, I remember sitting in the eighth grade math class and as Mr. Thibodeaux entered the classroom everything became hushed; you could literally have heard a pin drop. Mr. Thibodeaux, our new teacher, radiated a special presence. He emitted self-assurance and knowledge. I felt a kindly aura emanating from him, and although boisterous, his kindly no nonsense persona was always evident. Mr. Thibodeaux had short dark brown wavy hair, (he was obviously Cajun French), a ruddy complexion, stood about five foot five inches in height, had big feet, and was very stocky (fat). I have fond memories of Mr. Thibodeaux, my eighth grade math and science teacher.

While Mr. Thibodeaux liked me, there were lady teachers who did not, and they let it be known. When Miss Jordan, our Librarian and Miss Haas, my homeroom teacher and American History teacher, learned that, "that Ronnie Sonnier," was walking around the school halls with Barbara Miller they were appalled. The two teachers immediately tried to put a halt to our relationship. They called Barbara to the side and told her that she should not have anything to do with me, they said, "Ronnie Sonnier is trouble, you are too good a girl to have anything to do with him." And, they were right.

Miss Jordan and Miss Haas were right, I was not studious at all, and I got into a lot of fights. Barbara was an Assistant Librarian and a student in Miss Haas' history class. She studied hard, participated in class and made good grades. I knew as soon as I met Barbara that she was a wonderful person. Thanks be to Barbara's intuition, and I believe divine intervention, Barbara did not follow their advice, but stayed a true friend ever since the day her teachers tried to save her.

Miss Haas would recant her prior opinions of me many years later during a chance meeting with Barbara and me. We met her on the side of the road during a parade in downtown Ocean Springs, Mississippi. Barbara told her that I had just finished my Bachelors' Degree in Education from The University of Southern Mississippi (Miss Haas' alma mater; I had the same degree as Miss

Haas). To my surprise, Miss Haas said, "I am not surprised, I knew he could learn and make good grades."

Miss Haas went on to say, "It is the ones like Ronnie who can learn and participate, but they wasted their time, that bothered me most." She went on in a kindly way, "I suspected he had it in him, if he would only try." Miss Haas was the first teacher to teach me how to read correctly and learn.

When we saw Miss Haas, she had recently retired from teaching. She had an identical twin sister (they never married) that worked at the Biloxi Post Office, and Miss Haas told us that her sister was planning to retire soon. Miss Haas said that she and her sister planned to take a long vacation and travel to Europe.

Black and White Transition
"Transitions en noir blanc"

Biloxi, Mississippi, April 24, 1960, Bloody Sunday was by all accounts a dismal day in our history as black citizens of Biloxi planned an assault on the front beach. The air was expectant as though there was word received that a hurricane was approaching from the Gulf. All citizens felt apprehension that problems associated with integration plaguing the northern states was reaching Biloxi through sojourners who had plans and objectives to create chaos in Biloxi, especially on the otherwise tranquil sandy beaches. The sojourners, migrating economic parasites from the east and west coast and most especially Illinois, Pennsylvania and Ohio, were descending on Biloxi like Alexander on Tyrus.

Many citizens in Biloxi, of all diverse cultures, knew the meaning of storm warning. But, despite the warning of anarchy descending on our beaches, most citizens chose to ignore the newspaper and television coverage (which was scant to say the least) of the planned wade-ins.

The legend of the front beach incident is overblown hyperbole and practically no one except the black church ministers, provoking chaos by working and conspiring with The St. Paul United Church of Christ (formerly known as, The Evangelical and Reformed Lutheran Church) and their extension outreach services of The Back Bay Mission, expected any real physical altercations.

I vividly remember that a voice of the WLOX radio station did in fact relate a story of a fearful black youth. The black youth told the radio announcer, "I was told to stay home, lock my doors, and turn my lights off." He also said, "I was told to get down on the floor, get away from the windows." In other words stay away from the beach. WLOX aired a message from law enforcement that suggested all citizens should stay away from the beaches because of expected violence. I remember the broadcast and was stunned that a form of martial law was being enforced.

Reverend John Isgood (play on name), pastor of St. Paul's United Church of Christ, days earlier had planned, along with other white and black ministers, to organize and march in a group of 100 people (mostly black people, and I do not know where they were going to march). Many of these protestors ended up on front beach and would, from daybreak until the late evening, stoke fires for marshmallow and wiener roasts. The protestors enjoyed frolicking and occupying the beach for their pleasure (a beach privy to whites only by city decree). The protest was more like a sit-in in a segregated restaurant instead of an occupation of a beach.

The protestors left trash wherever they went. The City of Biloxi had to clean up the trash at taxpayer expense. The protestor's plans and actions kept residents and tourists away from the beach. Tourism was and is to this day, a paramount source of revenue for Biloxi and the Gulf Coast.

The front beach of Biloxi extends from near the old Tivoli Hotel on Pointe Cadet to a point near Pass Christian, Mississippi. The beach is more than twenty-five miles long, the shoreline of the Gulf of Mexico, and it runs along Old Highway 90. The beaches are across from many hotels and golf resorts which are the destinations for vacationers from many regions.

Along with a Dr. Mason, employee of the Biloxi Hospital located on the Back Bay of Biloxi, this clandestine assembly of blacks and whites intended to provoke a different beach decree from the Mayor and City Council of Biloxi. This assembly of persons wanted access to the beaches available to all who desired to use them.

As was usually the case with any event contrived by the infamous Dr. Mason and the childish and provoking Reverend Isgood, the planned protest, wade in, resulted in calamity and hate filled anarchy, the usual outcome of activities planned by these agitators. The agitators were fueled by their knowledge of the perceived success of the racial tensions and riots of 1919 in Chicago, Illinois provoked by The Chicago 9, a group of instigators and agitator students. The group of instigators and agitators were Community Organizers of their day.

Reverend Isgood and Dr. Mason were community organizers and were as silhouettes and or shadows on a backdrop as they agitated citizens to unrest from a car or bus, because they could. Neither of the community organizer agitators ever led from the front, but always from behind.

Dr. Mason was from upper Mississippi and had traveled, gaining northern exposure, and transferred his exposure and possible racial agitation experience to the Deep South. Mason had an obsession to gain notoriety and prestige at any cost.

Biloxi could not change fast enough to suit Mason and or Isgood, they were both egotistical narcissists supported by northern church affiliations. Biloxi's Division Street football stadium was one of their favorite gathering places for inciting black groups under the pretext of ministries.

(The U.S. Army Corps of Engineers began plans in 1952 to strengthen the beach and protect the seawall from washing into the Gulf of Mexico. Every storm and tidal change washed away the long shoreline.)

The NAACP would support Dr. Mason and Isgood's endeavors. It was and is true, blacks paid taxes and should have been able to enjoy the same privileges as all citizens. This was an ill-conceived civil rights agenda pushing the envelope for their personal political gain and not the rights granted by our United States Constitution or that of the sovereign state of Mississippi to go softly into the good night, peacefully without struggle, willingly as neighbors wanting the same outcome.

The beach agitators, elders and youth alike, were showing off by strutting and forming moving serpentine lines, slithering down front beach. These behaviors were not an intelligent demonstration of good citizenship. These actions were teaching the youth to provoke and agitate to gain their will, and these actions were damaging to any community or organization because it caused(s) long term malcontent with friends and foes marring history for purely selfish aggrandizement.

Mason's reputation suffered as he and his community organizer agitators sought to build his reputation into a formidable resume` of glowing medical and civil rights achievements. Mason was in fact a most indignant man, and certainly no gentleman. There would be several wade-ins and small progress with each such event causing law enforcement to seize potential weapons (there never were any weapons in evidence).

Mason himself would agitate from a distance staying away from direct law enforcement contact. He would organize the mostly black protesters, then split them into groups, near Biloxi Cemetery, the lighthouse and VA hospital, but would not physically protest or agitate with them. Mason instead led from behind and not in front as a leader should have done.

The reports of white citizens descending on an innocent, unprepared group of peaceful blacks was then and is to this day a complete distortion of historical facts. De-segregation of the beaches was much like integration of the public high schools in Biloxi, it was peaceful and a tribute to the entire diverse Biloxi citizenry (unlike the historical desegregation strife and anarchy of Little Rock, Arkansas). Assimilation.

Over the succeeding years Biloxi would change to a much more progressive, welcoming, inclusive diverse city with mostly liberal views, of which I have never approved. Barbara and I were stationed in Bamberg, Germany during the time from October of 1962 to October of 1964 (the Kennedy Assassination occurred on November 23, 1963), and things in the United States changed quite a bit.

The United States was changing, and Biloxi had gone from a quaint fisherman's village to a town of gambling casinos and higher crime. Biloxi is to this day, all inclusive, and culturally diversified, and this is good. Much credit could be attributed to Mason and Isgood laying a path with the 1960 Biloxi Beach wade ins and preparing citizens for desegregation of public schools on the Gulf Coast of Mississippi.

Biloxi Senior High School really did provide laudable leadership in calming the waters of possible racial strife. In 1963 students moved peacefully from previously all black Nichols High School (which was rundown and in much need of renovations; it did have the only swimming pool connected with a public school in Biloxi) to the previously all white Biloxi High School (which had no swimming pool) with no racial strife. This integration occurred peacefully to the credit of administrators, students, teachers, and understanding, cooperative and diverse parents. (Assimilation)

Barbara and I were married by Reverend Isgood in St. Paul's United Church of Christ on Back Bay in Biloxi (I might add that a casino is now in that location). We did not know or understand any of Isgood's outside activities for the church during that time, nor did we know or understand that this church was of the same affiliation as Reverend Jeremiah Wright's church in Chicago, Illinois (a church that teaches and supports Third World Black Liberation Theology). Barbara and I trusted and believed in St. Paul's United Church of Christ. The righteous indignation and holier than thou mentality which contributed to the exploitation of our family and other good Biloxi residents has left an indelible stain in its wake.

The people of Biloxi were not and are not bigots or prejudiced, we love our country. I thought back in the 1960's that I should begin a plan, and I should provide leadership to help bridge the gap between Cajun French and other cultures (and mentally I suppose I began taking notes for that transition).

I knew then that this bridging and healing would have to be accomplished through education and ruling by our Supreme Court, and so I have watched and made mental notes, then waited for an opportunity to begin. I believed then that Mississippi, Louisiana and or Texas would have to provide that necessary leadership.

While I was not sure in the 60's of the course of action to be taken, I did know that my own knowledge of education and desegregation of all public schools and colleges would help provide an avenue to equal education rights under the law. My plan then was to improve myself and my family while pursuing improvements through fair and reasonable enforcement of active laws pertaining to our education institutions. I knew then that I must find a path to and through Texas. Assimilation.

Cinderella Begins Her Escape
"Cendrillon commence sa Escape"

Carl Simmons, Barbara Miller Sonnier's Dad, was a ship fitter lead man for Litton Shipbuilding on the west bank of the Pascagoula River. Carl was rough cut and tough, but he treated me like a son. Carl died of cancer in the Biloxi VA Hospital and was buried on the VA grounds under the Giant Oak Trees Adorned With Spanish Moss. Carl was sixty-eight years of age. "I love you Carl," I said, and he replied as he lay dying at the VA Hospital, "I love you too, Ronnie."

Sally's mother, Evelyn Waltman Goff (Maw maw), passed away at the age of fifty-two. This left a teenage Barbara as the adult in the house caring for her family. Carl, seemingly oblivious to the meanness of Sally and the other children, was off working in the oil fields near Golden Meadows, Louisiana during all of Barbara's teen years.

Carl worked twelve hour days as a Pusher, ten days on and five days off, while Sally was a stay-at-home Mom. Sally was hard on both Barbara and I while we dated and grew up inseparably together seeing each other almost every day for several years. When Barbara and I were seventeen years of age, Sally caused a verbal altercation, because of the others (as I now call Barbara's siblings: Dianne Simmons Powell, Gail Simmons Galle, Karl Kent Simmons, and Joy Simmons Krohn; all born and currently living in and around Biloxi) complaining that Barbara was lying about their misbehavior while she and I watched (babysat) them for Sally to go out with her friends. A quarrel led to Sally slapping Barbara across the face and calling her a liar; this infuriated me. I told Sally not to hit Barbara anymore, and Sally ran me off yelling after me, "Don't come back."

I was told to never return (Carl was in Louisiana working), and this incident led to my joining the military at seventeen (a teenager as R. L. Miller had been when he enlisted in the Navy after an altercation involving his young wife, Sally Ann). I joined the US Army promising to return for Barbara.

Many years later Barbara and I would learn from a conversation with R. L.'s brother, J. T. Miller, Sr., Barbara's Uncle Sammy, that in mid-summer of 1943 Sally had had an altercation with her young husband, R. L. Miller, in the kitchen of his family home on Hoxie Lane. Sammy said that Sally had been very angry and had thrown a fork at him, Sammy, over a risqué verbal exchange. The fork stuck in Sammy's back.

The awesome sibling fistfight between Sammy and R. L., over something Sally had provoked, caused R. L. to angrily leave the house on Hoxie Lane that night, and soon afterward R. L. joined the US Navy. According to Barbara's Uncle Sammy, he and his brother R. L. would never say "I'm sorry to each other." The brothers would never see each other again. This tragedy has troubled Sammy Miller his entire life, at this writing he is in his eighties. Sammy Miller is a kind lovely man.

Pizza Pie

Later on in my life, my Mama did not work in the seafood factories; she worked in a shop that made fishing trawl, and or at Mary's Drive Inn making po'boys (sandwiches). Mama earned enough to help my Daddy, a civil service employee at Keesler Field, make ends meet. Sometimes Mama gave Joe (Mervin) a little cash for the two of us to share in buying pizza or burgers.

On one particular night, Joe and I joined forces with his best friend, Jack Kennedy McCarthy (no relation to JFK), and we drove around Biloxi in Jack's 1937 olive green two door Plymouth coupe. Jack was very proud of the car he had restored.

Joe, Jack, and Charlie McCarthy (not the ventriloquist, Charlie McCarthy) introduced me to pizza at Hugo's (Hugo's was a pizzeria near Keesler Field, the Air Force Base in Biloxi). Hugo's was situated on the corner of Division Street and Porter Avenue.

I refused to eat the pizza, and I said to the other guys, "That pizza looks like barf." "Eat a piece," my brother encouraged. Jack said, "Fold the pizza slice over like this." "Take a bite like this," Charlie McCarthy insisted, "It's delicious." I finally folded a piece of the pizza pie, and I ate it like a ravenous dog. From that moment on, one pizza was never enough for all of us.

Each time I was to join the group to ride around Joe had to ask Mama for extra money to spend. We would frequently pig out on pizza. The guys would all say, "It's our own fault, we shouldn't have forced him to take the first bite." Then they would all laugh. Sometime later....

The Big Train That Could Have
"Le Big Train qui aurait pu"

Joe and I had fun with Jack and Charlie's names, we often told other friends and our family that we knew Jack Kennedy and Charlie McCarthy personally. We four guys would drive around in the old '37 Plymouth, and on some night time escapades we would turn off the car lights to play Chicken (e.g. whoever screamed to turn the lights back on was Chicken).

On one particular night as we left a parking area in Ocean Springs, Mississippi, we turned the car lights off as we drove north, back toward Old Highway 90. After traveling about a minute, we all saw lights and heard a train whistle straight ahead in our path. Jack hit the brakes. We saw a train behind the light just as the Plymouth skidded front end into a deep trench next to the train track. I remember praying to God, "Our Father which art in heaven ...."

The train crossed on the track directly in front of the car. When the skidding car came to a stop we were pitched forward head first into the abyss. Fortunately, we had not reached the train tracks, and The Big Train That Could Have did not kill us.

In all of our stupidity, God protected us that night, and I believe we all felt his hand holding us for some other purpose. A very friendly old man, who looked like Walter Brennan, and walked with a limp like Walter Brennan (the actor, singer, songwriter), came to our rescue with his tractor and pulled us out of the trench (we discussed, where in the world had he come from, when we asked him, he would not say).

Shortly after that night, Joe and Jack joined the US Navy and Charlie joined the US Marine Corp. The only person in our group that I would see again, was my brother Joe (Mervin). I never saw the other guys again. I continued attending school and later joined the US Army.

There must be more than this, something somewhere, somehow more than this

Barbara Miller Arrives On My Radar Screen
"Barbara arrive sur mon eran radar"

Barbara, Sally Ann's daughter by R. L. Miller, the girl my Mama met at the beauty parlor came into my life. Barbara Miller and I met in the parking lot just outside Biloxi High School Football Stadium. Rebecca Miller was with her and both were dressed in red Biloxi Junior High Pep Squad uniforms. I was in the parking lot, at the front entrance to the stadium, in a car with my friend Hosie Parker. Hosie invited Barbara and Rebecca to ride with us to front beach and possibly get a drink at What-a-Burger.

Rebecca Miller stood about five foot four inches in height, had dirty blond hair and fair skin, hazel eyes, kind of plump, and possessed a very pleasant demeanor (we would be lifelong friends).

Barbara Miller had jet black curly hair and was about five foot six inches tall with a stocky build (not fat). Barbara was smart and beautiful. Barbara and I knew almost immediately that we were going to be inseparable and attached forever. I felt that I had always known her.

When I returned home that night, I related my encounter with Barbara to my Mama. I described Barbara to my Mama and she said, "Barbara is Sally Ann's daughter, the same girl I met at the beauty parlor last year. Remember I told you about meeting Barbara and her Mama."

I remembered the way Mama had described Barbara, and I remember that Barbara at that moment was My Soulmate. I believe then and now that I always knew Barbara was my partner for life.

"I Feel Your Soul Is Near"

As a child
When I first opened my eyes
and the fog began to clear,
I could see faces
but could feel your soul was not yet there.

All through the lonely years
as my fog began to clear,
I could see more faces
but could feel your soul
was not yet near.

Then one day
my fog began to lift,
and I could see you clearly
as you were,
and are today.

As I age my fog begins a slow return
and our rebirth draws near,
I know you will be beside me
as all becomes clear,
and I Feel Your Soul Is Near.

A Poem by: Rhone` Sonnier` Louviere`

There must be more than this, something somewhere,
somehow more than this.

Three Survived

"Trois survecu"

In her retirement somewhere outside of England the new Mrs. de Winter says "Last night I dreamt I went to Manderley again..."

Mrs. de Winter did not welcome her dream in the opening lines of the novel, "Rebecca," a murder mystery by Daphne Du Maurier. Mrs. de Winter and her husband, Maxim, first met in Monte Carlo, and our heroine lives in the present, reflects on the past, and contemplates the future. She is always in a dream like trance, meditating on a better life.

When the heroine (who is never named) revisits Manderley (Manderley is the burned down estate previously owned by she and her husband, Maxim) the huge gates open and she sees and describes the winding drive lined with Rhododendrons.

Book of Genesis, Chapter 26, Verse 3, King James Bible, Version 1611
Soiourne in this land, and I will be with thee, and I will blesse thee, and vnto thy seed I will give all these countries, and I will perform the oath, which I sware vnto Abraham thy father.

Soijourne - sojourner - soiourne - traveler - temporary resident - occupier - visit - stay – tarry

Espirit - the quality of being lively - mind - ghost – spirit

Book of Joel, Chapter 2, Verse 28, King James Bible, Version 1611
Your old men shall have dreams your young men shall have visions.

Book of Acts, Chapter 2, Verse 17, King James Bible, Version 16ll *Your young men shall see visions, and your old men shall dream dreams.*

In my own dream (Vietnam July 1962), the huge doors of a monstrous building begin to open, and I can see isle after isle of huts in a dark mist. There are oil lamps burning revealing a Vietnamese Village. People are moving about their business - some walking about, others eating, some building small skiffs to use for their fishing. All the children run and play and the unfortunate nightmare of human carnage from hand to hand combat unfolds.

Like Mrs. de Winter in "Rebecca," my dream is never a welcome one. My dream (now a composite dream) stays with me, wearing me down both physically and mentally, night after night, year after year, this is not a fond memory. My unique dream includes the memory of an incident with ten long dead soldiers and their apparitions or spiritual bodies.

These spirits are in full dress military gear (mostly olive drab fatigues with helmets, steel pots). The spirits sit, stand, and move about as supposed protectors, each waiting for something, anything different, but experiencing the same situation every night. The spirits gestures are in real time, but they are fluid, smoother, slow motion, dance-like (as in tai chi dance steps).

I have told my story as a one man act to over one hundred high school classes containing over one thousand students. I have told these students this story over a period of more than five years. I have determined that a storyteller must give considerable thought to presenting his necessary facts, truths, and or fiction. The storyteller should relate his information in such a manner that observers are entertained, and or educated by means of words, and or physical movements (such as martial arts movements, i.e., tai chi dance) to the fullest extent on every occasion that presents itself.

This story Three Survived begins with my performing tai chi moves (dance steps) expressing words of explanation for what is about to happen before their eyes accompanied by words for interested observers (usually a classroom full of students).

A certain amount of essential data must be placed in sequential order of events in order to prepare the minds of observers, the reason becomes clear and appreciated in its own time. While this unique story is not entirely true and or factual, it does depict an event, peoples, cultures, and a time in history. The story, My Story, is most often told by request of school administration or teachers to students in Language, American and or World History, Social Studies, Geography, High Math, Physics, Nursing, Biology, Drama, Dance, or Junior ROTC. This story may be told as fill when there is no prepared plan or curriculum left by the permanent teacher, and or with the prior approval of the same teacher.

Please be warned this story is not for the faint of heart and requires everyone in the room to be at least fifteen years of age and or a junior in high school. This story is highly inventive, imaginative, thought provoking, analytical, and a description of action and environment. The story reaches a crescendo of physical movements and sounds.

Many of the characters in this story are extremely harsh and demonstrative. An unwelcome disruptive and unknown spirit accompanies an element of fear which will raise the hair at the back (nape) of a person's neck. Observers have been known to leap from their chair and momentarily exit the room, however it is no more treacherous or macabre than Shakespeare's "Julius Caesar" or "MacBeth," or William Golding's "The Lord of the Flies," or F. Scott Fitzgerald's "The Great Gatsby."

Please be warned the story about to unfold or be told (often a one man standup performance in a small room) portrays a partial biography, some geography, some history, it includes some math, language, and martial arts dance steps. The story also includes some gruesome depiction of hand to hand combat, animal sounds and activities, possible spirit visitation, a bone chilling event sometime during the story telling, a shadowy elusive character with an exaggeration of creeping, crawling and slithering things.

As a substitute/guest teacher in Richland and Lexington counties in and around Columbia, South Carolina, I have taken to telling numerous stories to students concerning myself and certain animals vividly portraying the environment and specific events. This story helps to maintain order if for some reason there is not a curriculum plan for the day.

There are at least twenty books used in schools today which portray characters and events which eclipse with sordid macabre detail, unlawful actions and treachery more so than that of this story, the exception being that they are approved curriculum and part of a plan (no Holy Bible verses allowed).

Whether completely fact and or fiction (perhaps an invention of my active imagination which includes a warning of spirits and or an angel), I perform certain tai chi dance steps while relating a July 1962 Vietnam War story. I give an account of certain covert special operations of a contingent numbering thirteen or fourteen men skilled in various black martial arts abilities, each being bi-lingual, and of numerous cultural ethnicities such as Haitian, Jamaican, German, and or Israeli. The men are all dressed in olive drab military fatigues and wear black leather lace up high top boots.

While the harshness of the environment manifests itself, various other descriptions of key characters and relationships are described as life altering influences. Any or all names may necessarily be changed to protect The Storyteller and essential characters.

Descriptive Characteristics for the three main military characters in this story include:

Nickel - A twenty-five year old black Haitian male with short black closely cropped hair and a clean shaven face, muscular stocky structure, weight approximately two hundred and twenty pounds. Nickel stood six feet two inches tall, had great speed and coordination, an expert in weapons complimented by black martial arts expertise, tai chi.

Snicker - A twenty-seven year old black Jamaican male with buzz cut premature salt and pepper hair, muscular stocky stature; weight approximately two hundred and thirty pounds, great speed with his hand and feet co-ordination, an expert in weapons complimented by black martial arts expertise (tai chi). Snicker had huge beautiful white teeth with a prominent overbite; his large lips always framed his teeth in a grin (snicker). Snicker had a great booming voice that carried as though he spoke through a megaphone.

David - A twenty year old Caucasian (Black Irish coloring) who stood five feet ten inches tall and weighed approximately two hundred and ten pounds. David was a tree trunk of a muscular man, mean and fast (great hand and feet coordination) possessing a great dexterity with amazing agility. He was an expert in weapons, small arms fire, complimented by black martial arts expertise (tai chi, karate, judo and jujitsu). David's black prematurely graying hair was cut in a flat-top and he possessed an analytical genius and was known and respected as a critical thinking intellectual.

Pop - I am a white (Caucasian) male of French Acadian Cajun descent, born in Biloxi, Mississippi on February

13, 1944. I stand six foot two inches tall, have a cleft in my chin (genetic dimple), long torso, short legs, small hands with short fingers, small feet, clean shaven (now at 68 sporting a mustache). My hair is brown and cut in a straight back Latin style. I have hazel blue eyes and often walk aided by a cane.

When I walk I take short steps and most often have a balanced weight distribution with my feet anchored three feet deep in the ground (as in tai chi). I tend to be clumsy and appear distant (my thoughts somewhere other than where I am). I also have a hearing problem (due to military artillery) and quite often ask people to repeat themselves. In addition to assistance in walking and climbing stairs, the cane is often used as a prop, mock weapon when telling my story, Three Survived.

Book of Acts 2:17; Book of Joel 2:28; and Book of Daniel 1:17, King James Version of the Holy Bible *"The Day of the Lord....In The Last Days" - "It will come after this that I will pour out my spirit on all flesh and your sons and daughters will prophesy, your old men will dream dreams and your young men will see visions."*

In 1954, in Biloxi, Mississippi, I was about ten years of age and my brother was twelve. Joe and I attended St. Michael's Catholic School (Joe through seventh grade and myself through sixth grade). Most of our friends and associates attended public schools namely Dukate Elementary or Howard Number Two Elementary School. After students completed their education at these schools they progressed to either Sacred Heart for girls or Notre Dame for boys, and or Central Junior High School or Mary Michelle Junior High, then on to Old Biloxi High School on Howard Avenue (during mine and Barbara's high school years a new high school was built on Father Ryan Avenue).

After considerable deliberation and days of frustration, The Sisters of Mercy walked from St. Michael's School to

139

our home about a block away on 1st Street. The Sisters knocked on our front door and asked my Mama if they could speak to her concerning her two boys (my brother and I) and their apparent stupidity and lack of participation in school activities. My Mother answered them in her Cajun French dialect said, "Hello Sisters, *comens tal e vous*," or something in the order of "How are you Sisters? And, "Come in please." *("Comment allez-vous Sisters?" Et – "Entrez s'il vous plait.")*

Immediately the brightest Nun realized the problem my brother and I had was not stupidity, but lack of understanding of the English language. About this time other educators across America were, by happenchance, experiencing the same revelation.

Once The Sisters of Mercy realized this language situation certain means and methods were devised to remedy the root of the problem. Mercy came to my brother and I along with many other children hindered by their own unique language problems across the United States of America (particularly in Louisiana, Mississippi, Texas and South Carolina). Assimilation. Most of these children managed to obtain some semblance of an education each based on their individual abilities.

All these years it had been against the law to speak a foreign language in public schools and in many cases private schools as well. Across this nation parents had told their children to keep their mouths shut when approached for a response (answer) and simply nod your head up and down for yes; shake your head from side to side for no.

My brother Mervin managed to attend and complete Biloxi Senior High School with good grades; after graduation he joined the US Navy. I managed to attend and complete the eleventh grade. I left Biloxi Senior High School at the very young age of seventeen.

I had pestered my Dad to sign enlistment papers for me to enter the U.S. Army. I wanted to become a paratrooper (to my knowledge, I did not complete this training). I pestered my Dad for months, and he finally relented and wrote a letter (a letter of agreement to follow me) to the local Army Recruiter. This agreement allowed me to enlist. My Dad required a contract follow me while in the Army; this contract was to ensure that I would complete high school during my enlistment.

Upon enlistment the various forms of training and advanced training included time at Fort Chaffee, Arkansas and Fort Benning, Georgia, then with contingents of the Airborne and or Army Rangers at Dahlonega, Georgia.

In July of 1962 following months of exhaustive covert special training, I found myself in charge of and accompanied by twelve other military types waiting for assignment (Orders) from Camp P near Washington, DC to a place called Vietnam. Days passed while neither I nor any of the other military (all men) accompanying me were told why or for what purpose we would serve.

To my knowledge none of us were considered Airborne Ranger, or had earned any other respected and documented military distinction. We were covert and dark without a unit or distinct home. Possibly we were even rejects. We were told only that I was in charge of the soldiers for an essential strategic purpose with details to be divulged later.

"I do not want to be here," I thought, and I remember an ominous feeling of despair and pending doom. There must be more than this, something somewhere, somehow more than this.

We thirteen soldiers were never to exchange given names. Our thirteen member contingent was transported by covert means to Ron, Vietnam, then again by covert means to a compound/armory in a jungle like terrain near

141

The South Mekong River of Vietnam. Our mode of transport remains confidential to this day.

From the start, we were told that we were not to get well acquainted and mostly to keep our mouths shut and follow orders, "shut the bleep up" and do as you are told. I remembered Johnny and Son Illich and thought of what they had told me, "You will be OK in the Army, if you do what you are told and shut up and listen." Also, I reflected, these were almost the same words my Daddy told me (with less salty language) when he took me to the Trailways bus station on the beach in Biloxi. "You will be OK," Daddy said, as my bus departed with Biloxi in My Rearview Mirror.

Most of us slept a lot while others chose to read paperback books. I read "Rebecca" and "Frenchman's Creek," both novels by Daphne du Maurier; gothic novels by Phyllis Whitney and "Madam Castel's Lodger" by Frances Parkinson Keyes (the Keyes novel was about Civil War General Beauregard who was believed to be a member of The Illuminati, a sinister covert organization, of which Leonardo da Vinci had been an earlier member).

Day after day, after our arrival at the armory the discussion, scuttlebutt, turmoil, and grapevine was persistent and consistent surrounding missing rifles and the advantage these rifles would give our enemy. On several different occasions, upon visiting the mess hall for chow (the grapevine alive and well) we were informed over and over again, from both the grunts and noncommissioned officers alike, that one thousand (1,000) M16 rifles (*mille 1,000 fusils M16, French*) had been transported from the States, in fact arrived at this site and had been stored in this facility, as well, they had been entered in the Armory Stores Records and were now unaccounted for. This conversation, it seemed, was on the minds of everyone at this site, as well as, many in authority in the States. Military heads were already rolling and some would soon lose their rank.

142

On our fourth day on site, we met with The Brigadier General for the first time (no insignia indicating that he was a One Star General, the lowest rank for a General in the Army). The Brig was approximately forty-five years of age, six feet four inches tall and weighed about two hundred and thirty pounds. The Brig was in what seemed to be excellent physical and mental condition. For safety reasons, his safety that is, there were no salutes and we never greeted him as Sir.

During this first meeting, The Brig received us dressed like us in his olive drab bloused fatigues wearing black leather military boots and the ever present steel pot (he was accompanied by a young Vietnamese girl that he referred to as Girl). Establishing control, The Brig, dressed us down (inside a private shelter) and issued orders for a plan of action stating how we thirteen men would begin a thorough search of the armory and all quarters of personnel, commissioned and non-commissioned, for missing rifles.

The Brig said, "Pop, I want a damned plan from you for this mission." I had never written a plan and asked advice from some of the men, they laughed. Since there was no plan I figured correctly that any plan would draw skepticism and ribbing.

The only plan, not written, that I could think of was to reconstruct receiving of the weapons at the original reception point and have our men, all thirteen of us, comb every square inch of the armory, grounds, and terrain (roads and trails) within fifty miles of the site. When I verbally presented my plan to The Brigadier during breakfast the fourth morning after our arrival, he threw a tantrum and cussed worse than anyone I had ever heard curse in my young inexperienced life.

Shortly after throwing his tantrum, The Brig gave orders for everyone to cooperate with my simplistic plan (a personal insult to me). He said, "Pop, tell us your simple minded plan."

On the morning of the fifth day, I had the same results nothing (nada), and I had not been looking forward to reporting to The Brigadier, as he preferred being addressed. The Brigadier always sat in a recliner chair at the head of some makeshift tables covered by sky blue plastic. All other chairs were gray metal folding chairs with seat and back coverings of the same sky blue plastic covering bearing a symbol of a knight's headgear (The Blue Knight, *symbole d'un harnais Chevaliers*, this symbol most often used in jousting). There still had been no progress on the location of the rifles.

On the morning of the sixth day, we sat down for breakfast and were all expecting a thorough chewing out by The Brigadier. *Le Brigadier* immediately started into his usual tirade lambasting us, one by one, as we reported in and stated our findings, or lack thereof. It seemed that The Brig was saving me for last. Suddenly one of our men, code name David (a muscular in stature white kid, quiet, unassuming, analytical, and soft spoken had his eyelids blinking with his eyeballs rolling in their sockets) suddenly erupted with crazed laughter.

David suddenly grabbed the tablecloth, flung it back and off the table, dishes and food flew everywhere. The wooden boxes under the cloth had been painted sky blue, but we could easily read the stenciled inscriptions on the boxes giving the nomenclature of each box and their content. Initially, there was considerable celebration and then pandemonium as The Brigadier ordered everyone out of the area (he wanted us out of the entire compound. Everyone had to find another place).

No gratitude was ever shown for our success in finding the mishandled missing M16's. I believe, to this day, that no one wanted the truth to be known. The Brig appeared again along with the mysterious acting armed young Vietnamese girl.

One evening shortly after the discovery of the rifles The Brig told all of us to call him by his code name Lochinvar, and he proceeded to exquisitely recite a poem by the same name, and he told us that the poem was about a knight and a young maiden. We were told that Sir Walter Scott had written the poem. (The Brig's recital and character switch while reciting the poem worried me greatly.)

The Brig, Lochinvar, began reciting the poem in a deep voice, speaking in a song like fashion. The Brig appeared to become manic and extremely obsessed as he performed his narration. I do not believe that I was the only person that noticed this personality change. It was obvious that he had practiced this recitation (possibly before a mirror) and became euphoric in his delivery of the wonderful one man storytelling of "Lochinvar."

"Lochinvar"

By: Sir Walter Scott, published 1819

O, Young Lochinvar is come out of the west;
Through all the wide border his steed was the best;
And save his good broad-sword he weapon had none;
He rode all unarmed, and he rode all alone.
So faithful in love, and so dauntless in war,
There never was knight like the young Lochinvar.

He staid not for brake, and he stopped not for stone;
He swam the Eske River, where ford there was none;
But, ere he alighted at Netherby gate,
The bride had consented, the gallant came late:
For a laggard in love, and a dastard in war,
Was to wed the fair Ellen of brave Lochinvar.

So boldly he entered the Netherby Hall,
'Mong bridesmen, and kinsmen, and Brothers, and all;
Then spoke the bride's father, his hand on his sword,
(For the poor craven bridegroom said never a word,)
"O come ye in peace here, or come ye in war,
Or to dance at our bridal, young Lord Lochinvar?"

"I long wooed your daughter, my suit you denied,
Love swells like the Solway, but ebbs like its tide
And now I am come, with this lost love of mine,
To lead but one measure, drink one cup of wine;
There are maidens in Scotland more lovely by far,
That would gladly be bride to the young Lochinvar."

The bride kissed the goblet; the knight took it up;
He quaffed off the wine, and he threw down the cup.
She looked down to blush, and she looked up to sigh,
With a smile on her lips, and a tear in her eye.
He took her soft hand, ere her Mother could bar,
"Now, tread we a measure!" said young Lochinvar.

So stately his form, and so lovely her face,
That never a hall such a galliard did grace;
While her Mother did fret and her Father did fume,
And the bridegroom stood dangling his bonnet and plume;
And the bride-maidens whispered, "twere better by far
To have matched our fair cousin with young Lochinvar."

One touch to her hand and one word in her ear,
When they reached the hall door, and the charger stood
near;
So light to the croup the fair lady he swung,
So light to the saddle before her he sprung!
"She is won! we are gone, over bank, bush, and scaur;
They'll have fleet steeds that follow," quoth young
Lochinvar.

There was mounting 'mong Graemes of the Netherby
clan;

Forsters, Fenwicks, and Musgraves, they rode and they
ran.
There was racing and chasing on Cannobie Lea,
But the lost bride of Netherby ne'er did they see.
So daring in love, and so dauntless in war,
Have ye e'er heard of gallant like young Lochinvar?

The man, now known as Lochinvar sat back in his recliner shoulders back and chest out; he was obviously preening for his captive audience. I thought he did quite well actually, but there was no applause or any other acknowledgement of a poem well presented. We all had to respect his rank, that was a given, but I do not believe anyone liked him, I for one, certainly did not like him. I did not trust him in the least. I felt a foreshadowing of dark events.

Lochinvar, The Brig, stayed clear of us for a couple of days after his fine performance. The day and time came when Lochinvar told us that our new mission was to evacuate large buildings inhabited by Vietnamese fisher and boat people. Lochinvar said the Viet people, after British and French occupation, had taken over these shelters. Through the ensuing twenty years they had settled in the barracks and storage buildings making them their homes.

Our orders (13 member contingent) were to peacefully ask these Vietnamese people to evacuate the premises which were to become American Forces and Allied quarters. As we were leaving the Armory, Lochinvar said to us, "There are thirty foot long crocodiles where the Red Mekong River and the South Mekong River join." Lochinvar continued looking me in the eye, "Pop, the Viet villager guides tell us that those crocodiles like to eat Frenchmen."

Very early the next morning (around two a.m.) we (all thirteen of us) received confirmed orders; the assignment which would alter our lives forever. Lochinvar then took his parting quip saying, "There are crocodiles thirty feet long where the Red Mekong River and the South Mekong River join." He said to me once more for emphasis, "Pop, the Viet villager guides tell us those crocodiles like to eat Frenchmen."

At this point, The Brig knew his image and control of the Armory lost and found M16 rifles was questioned by his superiors, and The Brig was covering his tracks. Through the grapevine, our thirteen man team was told that The Brigadier, Lochinvar, was called to headquarters, never to be heard of again.

(Shortly thereafter, we approached our destiny with blind optimism.)

The Brigadier had left one last order; we were to leave the encampment immediately and proceed to evacuate the Viet occupied buildings fifty miles away. We were to find this site using verbal instructions from The Brig's liaison (we had no map).

Our thirteen member contingent was transported from the compound by covert means to a site of extremely dense jungle terrain of The South Mekong River (this is the location where it joins The Red Mekong River of North Vietnam). We traveled by day through terrain that was unfamiliar and very foreign to us. There were tall green trees, hanging vines, and dense large leafy foliage.

The people that we did meet would avoid getting near us and never spoke to or greeted us in any way; they actually shunned us. As we were moving along the people seemed to emerge from holes in the ground. There were unfamiliar animal sounds; the strange sounds were terrifying to us in their loudness, ferocity and frequency. The jungle sounds would sometimes become silenced by our own noisy movements.

Using what information and descriptions we had, we finally arrived at our destination prepared to get some well-deserved rest and relaxation before approaching the task we had been assigned. We had been told to evacuate all buildings and premises within approximately ten miles of the known center. The center was to be determined by us and not by the current inhabitants. The inhabitants were not hospitable and avoided us as we entered the largest of the buildings in the village.

We approached and attempted to befriend the people with various rations, smokes, and chocolate bars. The villagers would not speak, but gestured angrily with their hands that we must not remain; we were not welcome and must leave. The inhabitants spoke in a low whispering guttural language, perhaps some sort of indecipherable Vietnamese or Chinese dialect which none of us could understand. The Vietnamese villagers were quickly becoming very hostile, and I felt they were on the verge of violence. Trembling with fear and foreboding, I bent down on one knee to give a very small girl child a chocolate bar (Hershey, I think).

Suddenly, I was terrified as the hair at the nape of my neck felt electrical and spiked like that on the back of an angry dog. It was then that I clearly remembered hearing my parents tell me, and I could hear them speaking to me, "Keep your mouth shut, pay attention, and listen carefully." All of a sudden, from a sinister calm came calamity accompanied by a blood curdling scream a word - moo auhr TAY - a high shrill sound that literally and physically scared the crap out of me (Vietnamese villagers eyes were bugging with recognition and fear...).

Almost simultaneously I heard another scream and saw, in my peripheral vision, a whitish gray blur moving quickly. The figure ran past and across in front of me; the warrior was moving toward one of my men. The warrior wore heavily soiled ratty looking grayish brown pajamas. The clothing had many tears, holes and patches merging into each other. In the warrior's outstretched, but partially bent left arm, he was wielding what appeared to be a very sharp formidable machete (made of bamboo, as I recall). I saw, as though in slow motion the outreached hands and arms of this very lean and miniature old person who was about to decapitate Snicker.

At the time I heard *moo auhr tay*, I knew the word, the terrifying sound and the meaning of the word was "Kill," "Murder," "Death." I remembered the word from somewhere in my own past. After hearing the word, I instantly forgot the word. From that moment on, I remembered only the word the old man screamed and it was definitely something to do with murder.

I thought, "There must be more than this, something somewhere, somehow more than this. J'ai pense: "Il doit y avoir plus que cela, quelque chose quelque part, en que sorte plue que cela."

I felt danger and simultaneously I came up from kneeling on my right knee while my right hand grabbed my bayonet (*baionette* from French for knife) from my ankle scabbard (sheath for holding a sword or knife). I gripped my bayonet firmly as I lunged forward and up aiming my knife for the warrior's left shoulder. To my shock, I missed terribly. I had driven the point of the long knife into the left side of the warrior's neck with extreme and deadly force. The force of my lunge had lifted the warrior into the air knocking him off of his feet. I watched as he came back down settling on both feet, and he immediately began shaking like a loosely jointed Raggedy Ann Doll being shaken and mauled by a ferocious pit bull.

All of a sudden, it seemed that evening had arrived and there was little light except from oil lamps now becoming visible. We saw what appeared to be hundreds of lighted oil lamps in small hut like bamboo shelters constructed along the walls and within the confines of the large building.

I became aware of the warrior's entire body convulsing, as my entire body convulsed along with his. His blood curdling cry turned into a purring and gurgling sound. His blood spurted high in the semi-darkness toward the unseen ceiling and all around us outward into the surrounding darkness, spraying all within range.

I thought, "There must be more than this, something somewhere, somehow more than this."

Suddenly there was pandemonium and overwhelming panic. All hell broke loose. We were engaged in hand to hand human fighting. There was kicking, biting, gouging, screaming, hollering, and then after an indeterminable time a scary silence, no sounds, not even animal sounds. I remember at this point I wet myself. I soiled myself messing in my underwear and fatigues. I knew that I was wet all over my body with something sticky and I stunk.

I thought, "There must be more than this, something somewhere, somehow more than this, and I prayed.

Our weapons were not loaded (the Army did not allow us to lock and load), and they (what appeared to be a hundred people) had farming and fishing implements. Oil lamps started going out as silhouettes and shadows haunted the walls of the monstrously large building.

Nos armes n`ont pas ete charges et ils (ce qui semblait etre une centaine) avaient agriculture et pecheen en ceurve.

Lampes a huile a commence a sortir sous forme de silhouettes et les ombres hantent les murs de la nonstrueusement grand batiment.

I remember thrashing around kicking, biting, and hitting with my fists and feet. I lashed out at anything that touched me, perhaps some of my own men. Something or

151

someone hit me very hard, and I passed out cold falling onto my back. I woke up sometime later and it was dark in the large building. I had heavy weights lying across my chest and legs. The weight was smothering me; I could not feel my legs; I could not breathe; I felt as though I was suffocating, dying.

I thought, "There must be more than this, something somewhere, somehow more than this."

I felt wetness all over my body and remembered that I had soiled myself. I immediately recalled the blood and the killing. I said aloud to myself, "This is my blood, I have been wounded." All of a sudden, I heard shushing sounds, "Shhh hush," - "Quiet," - "Listen," - "Don't move;" and I heard other sounds of thumping, thuds, whacking, stabbing, and guttural human sounds. I remember thinking, "Sounds, all these sounds usually mean pain or worse." Darkness overcame me once more.

Once more, I woke up in a trance, and I could hear gunfire and screaming. I began to understand the sounds, men (perhaps two, I thought) that were lying on top of me, and I screamed for them to get off of me. I thought of Abe Goff and strained with all my might, but my straining was to no avail; I could not move the men; I had no strength. I was being smothered and shouted, "Get off of me." In unison both of the men lying on top of me said said calmly and quietly, in a soft hush, "Be quiet," - "Shhhh," - "Listen," - "Do as you are told!"

The whacking sounds started again, and I realized that people with weapons were attacking us. I knew that I had not been hit by weapon fire, but I soon learned that the men on top of me were being slaughtered. I quickly shut up and the attacks stopped. The darkness and minimal light with shadows and silhouettes became apparent for the first time, at this point I fainted.

When I woke up again I became very nauseated and threw up on myself and the two guys on top of me. The stench of blood, vomit and human excrement overwhelmed us. The soldiers made noises as we all were attacked over and over again, and I realized that I had never been hit, but the men on top of me had been injured, or worse. I wanted to be somewhere else, anywhere but here.

I thought, "There must be more than this, something somewhere, somehow more than this, and then I knew that I was not alone."

My sense of self-preservation began clicking in as I became aware of what I believed to be our life's blood (literally and figuratively) oozing, draining and spilling over each other. Our blood intermingling as we American Soldiers became united as American Indians would say "We Became Blood Brothers." I innocently remembered witnessing the cutting of one thumb and then another as two young boys pressed their cut thumbs together creating The Bonds of Brotherhood. I thought, "That warm liquid is blood pouring over me, drenching my already saturated fatigues, and I knew that the blood was dripping onto the already wet floor."

We are finished I thought in English - caput, I thought nervously in German - and, *fini* (the end) I thought humorously, where there was no humor, in French.

I thought, "*Fini,* or maybe a new beginning," I continued in my thoughts….

The Book of James, Chapter 1, Verse 17 (King James Version of the Holy Bible) -
Every good gift and every perfect gift is from above and cometh down from the Father of lights, with Whom is no variableness, neither shadow of turning."

I thought, "There must be more than this, something somewhere, somehow more than this."….."Il doit y avoir

153

plus que cela – quelque chose quelque part – en quelque sorte plus que cela."…

I awoke once again as though from a trance. I slowly came to my senses, but I started trembling uncontrollably. My body was racking with deep sobs - sobbing - sobbing - sobbing - and, I was thinking, "What am I doing here?" - "How could this happen to me?" - "Why did my Mama and Daddy let this happen to me?" - "I do not want to be here!" - "I want to be somewhere else." All these thoughts ran quickly and clearly through my mind.

In my mind, I cried out for Barbara, my soulmate, but she was not there, and she did not come. I thought, "Someone else will come, someone will save us, save me." "God," I thought and prayed selfishly under my breath, prayed to be saved. *Dieu, pensai-je. J'ai reflechi et prie sous mon soufflé pour etre sauve.*

No one came, I felt hopeless for us, all of us, all of us that might be left alive. *I thought again, "There must be more than this, something somewhere, somehow more than this."…… "Il doit y avoir plus que cela - quelque chose quelque part - en quelque sorte plus que cela."……*

Somewhere in my mind I found the courage to think and then softly speak to the two men on top of me, "Leave me, get away from here as fast as you can." I told them, "I cannot feel my legs, I cannot move." Again, I tried lifting the two men off of me, (like Abe lifted the front end of the milk truck on the Biloxi Ocean Springs Bridge many years ago). My efforts were futile. I thought that they must have fallen on me and were now protecting me.

At this point I realized, from recollection of voices and dialect, that the men on top of me were Snicker (the Jamaican) and Nickel (the Haitian). I remembered that they were both black. I thought, "I will never know their real names."

"Forget me, save yourselves," I said to Snicker and Nickel. I was thinking, "They are protecting a Brother Soldier." In unison they said, "Please, please be quiet." "Shhhhh, be quiet and listen," Snicker said.

Again, I heard footsteps, hacking sounds, whacking sounds, thud sounds, and grunts coming from Snicker and Nickel. I could hear shuffling feet and running sounds, fighting noises all around us. I heard and understood different languages, and I could understand words, but I could not link them into sentences to understand what was taking place. Loud screaming and gunfire was continuous in the background. My fear increased.

Suddenly, it became calm and silent in the midst of the storm, our turmoil. I heard animal sounds, all kinds of animal sounds. I heard growling, howling, and barking sounds. I thought, "Gumbo is that you, Gumbo." My thoughts took me all the way back to when I was five years of age, back to the chomping sounds that I heard as an alligator ate my dog Gumbo.

I was terrified. Once again, I thought I could hear a chattering sound, and I realized it was coming from me. I was making guttural sounds, a whimpering sound, and I was gnashing my teeth. More panic set into my very heart and soul, my inner most being. I was perhaps experiencing death throws.

I heard screaming coming through the doorways of the warehouse. I could hear people shouting loudly, "Crocodiles!" "Crocodiles!" Run, Run, Run, "Crocodiles!" I could hear reptilian slithering and clapping sounds, and I suddenly realized with great fear that Lochinvar (The Brig) had not been lying to us about crocodiles. I thought, "If I ever needed to change into Boy, son of Tarzan, it is now."

I remembered the last words from Lochinvar (The Brig), he had said, "There are crocodiles thirty feet long where the Red Mekong River and the South Mekong River join." Lochinvar spoke directly to me, "Pop, the Viet villager guides tell us those crocodiles like to eat Frenchmen."

"What the hell," I thought, I had dealt with an alligator eating my dog Gumbo when I wasn't even five years old, I can deal with this." I continued thinking, "How damned bad can they be?"

Book of Luke, Chapter 13, Verse 28, King James Bible, Cambridge Edition *There shall be weeping and gnashing of teeth, when ye shall see Abraham, and Isaac, and Jacob, and all the prophets, in the kingdom of God, and you yourselves thrust out.*

I could smell excrement and the sourness of animals, and I urinated on myself again, and I fainted once more.

It seemed like days, not hours, had passed when I saw Silhouettes - Shadows - and, Soft Lights. I saw what I thought to be a huge man. The man was approximately six foot four inches tall and possessed a thick body. I (we) could see a vision, and I (we) perceived a dark eerie feeling accompanying the shadow of a man, a soldier, wearing what appeared to be bloused fatigues and a steel pot (helmet, like ours).

The man continued approaching us out of the darkness, drifting closer and closer in what appeared to be a cloud that was surrounding him. Within the cloud (heavy mist) were soft lights pulsating from a rainbow behind and over him. (At this point, the man was about ten feet from us.) There were no accompanying movements or sounds as the man moved closer to us. (He was now five or six feet from us.) I could have sworn that he said, "Ronnie." "Naghhh!" I thought. My next thought was that it was my old friend, Charlie McCarthy (Jack Kennedy McCarthy's younger brother, but I immediately thought it could not be).

As the man came closer the lights diminished and I noticed once more his size, and that he appeared to have a huge hunch back. He came closer and closer to us kneeling down on his right knee; then he cautiously raised himself up to an almost erect position. He looked about the entire room slowly and deliberately. Then he cautiously bowed his body at the waist as he drew closer to us. When the man was only a foot or two away from our faces he spoke in a hushed, but clear voice, "Shhhh, be quiet, listen, wait." "Shhh, be quiet, be quiet, shhhh, listen, wait shhhhhhhh," he said this over and over.

Book of Daniel, Chapter 1, Verse 17, King James Version of The Holy Bible *"As for these four children, God gave them knowledge and skill in all learning and wisdom: and Daniel had understanding in all visions and dreams." Fort cris et des coups de feu a ete continue dans le fond comme plus de peur mis po tout a coup, il est devenu silencieux – et le calme est venu au milieu de la tempete (notre trouble).*

En ce qui concerne ces quatre enfants, Dieu leur a donne la connaisance et l`intelligencedans toutes d`apprentissage et de sagesse, et Daniel expliquait toutes les visions et les reves.

I reflected back to my boyhood, and I remembered the comfort of my home in Sea Coast Camps. Silhouettes, shadows, soft lights, and a sense of peace fell over me as though someone had placed a comforting cover over us. I thought, "Someone is covering our backs." All of a sudden it occurred to me that I had experienced a vision, a vision of a really big person.

"I can't believe this," I thought, but I knew it to be a reality and not some kind of apparition. I heard static sounds coming from the soldier's direction. I likened the sounds to sporadic static electricity. I was terrified by and of him, and of the sounds and lights seemingly created by him.

It became very quiet again. No sound at all, no static. Snicker broke the silence by asking me to find out the kneeling man's name. (At this time the soldier was still one to two feet from us.) "Pop, ask him his name," Snicker had said. I answered Snicker with, "Are you nuts, you ask him yourself."

I thought to myself, "Wait for what, who?" At that moment, I first felt that I knew this man, but could not recall or bring to mind the name of this kindly phantom (an angel). "Naghhh! I thought, this is not an apparition." *C'est alors que j'ai senti que je connaissais cet home mais ne pouvait pas placer le nom de cette bonte.*

The deafening silence became very eerie and my temporary feeling of safety at the arrival of the apparition/soldier soon vanished. Time seemed to stand still and after what seemed like an eternity the floor of the large building suddenly began to tremble. As the entire building shook and things fell around us, and on us, very bright piercing lights appeared in the trap door style windows and through cracks in the ceiling.

Things that appeared to be spiders were hanging from lines. The lines and things were being lowered toward us from above. I thought that I was hallucinating (I had been coming in and out of consciousness since being knocked out). I thought that maybe I was suffering from shell shock or something as I watched the shadowy creatures appear. The creatures appeared to be on the walls, and they were also landing on the floor directly in front of me (us). The creatures crawled and slithered about, side to side, bobbing up and down while moving ever closer to me (us) as they yelled names, code names, our names. There were no replies, as the creatures moved about, getting closer to me (us), continuing to call our code names.

I heard someone call, "Nickel." Nickel lifted himself off of me. As Nickel raised his body he stretched out his arms and yelled, "That's me." As I felt his weight shift off of my body, my legs were freed (they had been trapped by Nickel's weight). *Je sentais le poids deplacer hors de mon corps comme Nickel souleve hors de moi – son bras etendu. C'est moi crier.* I heard Nickel shout, "Here I am, here I am," *"Me voici, Nickel cria a nouveau.*

As the creatures raised Nickel off of me (us), I witnessed other creatures reach The Phantom Soldier, the one who had been the first to come to our rescue. The Phantom Soldier was not moving or talking to anyone, and I felt very sad and very sick. I felt my body trembling, shuddering, and I was sobbing. I was in a crying jag and could not stop trembling. I thought to myself, "I am tired of this crap; I have had all that I am going to take," and I chuckled out loud." *"Je suis fatigue de cette merde j'ai pense, J'ai eu tout ce que je vaid reposer pendant, et je en riant."*

While crouching beside the The Kneeling Phantom Soldier, the creatures spoke quietly in undertones and made mournful sounds as they solemnly shook their heads from side to side. The creatures' bodies shook as they cleared their throats (one creature leaned away and wretched uncontrollably).

The creatures removed a hump from off The Kneeling Phantom Soldier's upper shoulders and back thus changing The Hunchback of Notre Dame illusion of the soldier. Our Phantom Soldier with the hunchback had died in a kneeling position about five or six feet from where we lay. *Ils ont enleve une bosse de dessus de ses epaules et le dos superieur en mutation "L'Le Bossu de Notre-Dame" elution.*

"What the hell is that stench?" I heard one of the creatures say, as he stepped back and regrouped and calmed himself (perhaps he had realized it was me that was stinking so badly). At this point, the creatures began to roll The Phantom Soldier, our Angel, our Hero, our Spirit, onto a makeshift stretcher.

The Phantom Spirit was dead and had remained in a protective kneeling position, rifle still gripped in his hands, he was still wearing his steel pot. On the stretcher he remained in that position as they covered him with an olive drab wool US Army blanket. As the creatures slowly disappeared into the darkness they carried Our Protector with reverence. *Les creatures emmenerent lentement et avec respect, comme ils out disparu dans l'obscurite. Espirite de corp. Semper phi (Semper Fidelis,* Latin for Always Faithful or Always Loyal), and I thought, "Good Stuff, really Good Stuff."

I was wakened from my thoughtful escape, brought back to reality by more excited and louder calling of code names. The code name calling continued as the creatures (I called them this in my mind) crawled around in the building on all fours moving what appeared to be ragged lumps. I could hear some name calling coming from the open side windows, but no answers ever came. Near me, inside the building, the movement and stirring became frantic.

After Sometime, it seemed to be about an hour, I heard a nearby voice call another name. "Snicker," I heard the voice shout. "Here I am," Snicker shouted very loudly, and I heard movement toward us. "Here I am," he said, raising himself as high as he could, arms and hands extended. Snicker's weight left me, and I could breathe again, but not very well.

I said to the creatures, "I am Ronnie Sonnier, I am an Army soldier," but got no reply. It registered with me that for some unknown reason the creatures had handled

Nickel and Snicker with less reverence than they had The Phantom Soldier. I heard other names, but not mine. Someone called, "Mercury!" No reply. Someone called "Pluto, then Saturn!" No reply. Other code names were called, no replies. I did not remember their names. I became totally silent.

I heard more creatures shout, "Pop!" I did not identify with who that could be. Once again I heard someone call, Pop! I wondered, Why aren't they calling Ronnie or Sonnier." I did not hear my name. *J'ai entendu les créatures crier "Pop!" et ne s'identifient pas a qui cela pourrait etre. "Pop!" et je me demandais quand ils appellant "Ronnie," ou "Sonnier" - mais ils n'ont pas.*

I saw three more creatures shaking their heads side to side as they approached me. The three of them threw an Army blanket over me and hoisted me three feet or so above the floor. The creatures thought that I was dead, and they grabbed me to remove my body from the building.

"I am not dead," I said. The creatures dropped me, I was hurt again. As they backed away from me I said, "I am not dead." They replied nervously and in unison, "We can see that. "What is your name?" I replied with my Regular Army Number, 55555555.

They said, "Not good enough soldier, that isn't what we need, you have to remember and say it." I was stricken with panic, and I reflected on my training. I thought, "What in hell, then it came to me." "Pop! That's me," I shouted as I reached for the open welcoming arms of the creatures. *"Qu'est-ce en enfer." Pensai-je. Puis il est venu à moi. "Pop!" C'est moi j'ai crie, atteignant pour les bras ouverts accueillants de "Les Créatures."* I said again and again, caught in the exhilaration of being saved, "I am Pop!, I am Pop!, I am Pop!, that's me, I am Pop!"

The creatures carrying me away from the large building cradled me in their arms like a new born baby; they also told me who they were and where they had come from. I knew them to be Marines, they didn't tell me this, but I knew they must be Marines. I was to find out later that I was partially correct. They were US Calvary and Marines with medical gunship helicopters sent to find us and bring us to the USS Roosevelt. I thought, "The Marines to the rescue." I would later learn The Roosevelt was in the Mediterranean waiting to render further assistance.

The Marines were moving fast carrying me between them, one Marine at my feet and the other at my shoulders. We left the soft ominous lights and atmosphere of the big building through the giant gates. As we sped through the jungle our eyes needed time to adjust because it was pitch black outside. We suddenly crashed into a tree or something and fell to the ground. *Les Marines ont été en mouvement rapide me portant entre eux un à mes pieds et une autre à mes épaules. Il était à l'extérieur complètement noir et nous avons accéléré à travers la jungle. Nous avons soudainement percuté un arbre ou quelque chose et tomba sur le sol.*

I was splayed on the ground, hurt again. The two Marines scooped me up and started running, as best they could, toward the lights of waiting helicopters. As they ran my body was swinging between them. *J'ai été ecrases sur le sol blesser a nouveau – et ils m'ont ramasse et a commence a courir quemieux qu'ils pouvaient avec moi balancer entre eux vers les lumieree d'helicopteres d'attente.*

I thought, "There must be more than this, something somewhere, somehow more than this."

As we approached a helicopter the Marines reared back and then forward pitching me up and through the massive door of the helicopter. I became partially faint as I struck the hard surfaces inside the helicopter. I slid on the rough floor and landed in an almost sitting position against an equally hard bulkhead. I wondered how I could slide on such a rough surface.

I lay in the helicopter swooning, going in and out of consciousness, semi-consciousness, somewhat like a drunken stupor. As I awakened from that deep stupor I could see men lining the walls of the helicopter. The men were lying about on the floor in various repose; they all appeared to be dead. "I am not dead," I remember thinking.

The helicopters were roaring, their blades accelerating as the Sailors and Marines began hustling about preparing to get out of Vietnam. I thought to myself, selfishly and briefly, "The helicopter motors were humming and the propellers were turning, ready to fly me away from Vietnam."

As the great helicopter started moving, I grabbed hold of a person and something on the hard bulkhead. I was holding on for dear life as the helicopter left the ground accelerating forward, then rolling (right I felt), and jettisoning forward to, I believed, the Roosevelt. As the helicopter rolled right, I saw a soldier with his face swelling up as it became distorted, and I saw a rat exit his mouth and run across the floor then jump out the helicopter door. *Comme il a roulé à gauche, j'ai vu un soldat avec son gonflement du visage-up car il est devenu déformé et un énorme rat est sorti de sa bouche, puis a couru à travers le sol en sautant par la fenêtre.*

The soldier (a genuine hero, I thought) rolled toward the door and flew out into the night, down toward the dense dark in country jungle below. Unfortunately, I did not recognize him. He was gone; he flew out of my sight, down-down-down into the in country of Vietnam. I remember feeling sorry for him. I thought, "I feel sadder for his loved ones back home, stateside, or wherever home might be."

I could feel intense heat and see a great brightness emerging from an ominous darkness. The monstrous warehouse was burning as the US Calvary contingent was flying out our living and dead. The blaze grew as the copters carrying some of my men and me lifted off and turned heading toward the South China Sea and then to the USS Roosevelt (Rosie) in the Mediterranean. I looked out through the dense smoke, and I could see the flames licking the heavens above the trees. The flames reached over one hundred feet into the sky and outward around the building another hundred feet. The warehouse was collapsing in on itself with more yellow than red at the center, a "Dante's Inferno." And, I remembered the Fire in Rayne from my childhood.

I made it out of Vietnam alive, but with an undefined, undiagnosed repeating fever along with some kind of mental anxiety and accompanying depression disorder, shell shock as they routinely called it back then (PTSD now). I was told by medics and mental examiners, of all types, that most of what I remembered and ranted and raged about never happened.

I was having a horrible time adjusting and felt as though no one understood or cared. I felt dismissed every time I told my story, from my vantage point and not that of my rescuers. "Take an aspirin, and I'll see you in the morning soldier," they basically said. "Get back to your duty as soon as possible," they told me politely but dismissively.

My body was examined in and out by many very good medics and some doctors. I had not been scratched in Nam, all that blood belonged to others, probably Nickel and Snicker. *Je n'avais pas été rayé de la Nam, tout ce sang appartenait à d'autres.*

Other than that, I became just one more of tens of thousands of normal grunts stationed in Germany. I do not clearly remember my trip to Germany. In late

164

September of 1962, I was joined in Bamberg, Germany by my wife, my soulmate, Barbara. We lived off base on the economy. Our first apartment was on Adam Saenger Strasse across from the backyard of a large Catholic Church. The church had beautiful bells that sounded quite often. We enjoyed our small attic apartment.

(It was years before I shared anything about Nam with Barbara. I felt some shame; I do not know why. Some details Barbara discovered as I wrote this book and she edited my writing.)

Our daughter Scarlett (my Princess) was born on July 3, 1963. We were happy kids. Shortly after Scarlett's birth, we moved to a small house closer to the Main Gate of the Post. Two of our military friends, Gene and Marge Knoploh, lived in that area; they were a little older and more mature than us. Gene and Marge had a red Volkswagen bug which we bought from them when they returned to the states (Iowa).

President John Kennedy was assassinated on November 23rd, 1963. This was not a good day for Barbara or me and most especially the assassinated President of The United States of America, John Fitzgerald Kennedy. I remember I had to pull guard duty the day (night in Germany) that the President was assassinated in Dallas, Texas. We were all scared. Our German neighbors were stunned and fearful at what might happen in the world, in Germany and in turn to them.

We made it through those days and struggled as did most through the experiments of various Presidents. We endured the horrors of the Vietnam Conflict which turned into The Vietnam War. The Vietnam War cost many thousands of lives, on both sides, over many years.

(Since the 1970's, Cajuns have exhibited renewed pride in their heritage and consider themselves a valuable national resource. Cajun music and food have become accepted and enjoyed by America.)

Over the ensuing years, Barbara and I traveled extensively with my employment. We held various jobs, and we devoted our time to rearing our four children. Our family did everything together. (Barbara and I had no idea that our family would become dysfunctional. We never thought that we might be creating a dysfunctional family. We were just rearing a family.) Getting jobs was no problem but keeping them was a problem for me. I never was much of a social animal as I performed favors, and owed favors.

During the years that we moved with my employment, I frequented many different VA hospitals. While we lived in Woodlawn, Virginia, I would periodically travel to the Salem VA Medical Center in Salem, Virginia. At this point in time, more than thirty years had passed since I was in Vietnam.

On one particular day as I walked toward the emergency entrance of the VA hospital in Salem, I heard a familiar distinctive booming voice. I walked closer to a group of Vets sitting outside the hospital (I walked slowly, slowed by my injured aging legs and assisted by my cane).

Some of the Vets were shouting and bantering playfully with another Vet that they were helping out of a wheelchair. Some of the Vets had lost an arm, a leg, or both (all of them had mental conditions). "I'm tired of the same old war story old man," one of the Vets said to the man that they had helped out of the wheelchair. "I'm tired of your bull....," the Vet continued. "But it's true," the Vet being assisted argued with his booming voice.

"Nickel told all of you the same story," and it is true I tell you, the Vet boomed. As they sat him beside some of his old cronies on the park bench, the old Vet grinned and that is when I knew for certain it was him.

"Is that you Snicker?" I asked. The Vet looked up in shock and recognition as though he had seen a ghost. He asked, "Pop, is that you?" The other Vets shouted out, "You old SOB, you have been telling the truth!" Snicker tried to raise himself to his feet, but he had forgotten that he had only one leg (Snicker had lost his right leg from injuries incurred way back when).

Snicker yelled obscenities beyond the capabilities of any sailor. "You white Cajun bas......" he said. Snicker shouted in anger, "You sorry white honkey SOB! You caused all this. It's your damned fault!" It took all of us to eventually calm him down. Snicker finally stopped grumbling and cursing me over our past and said, "I love you."

Snicker told me that Nickel had died three weeks prior at the Salem Medical Center, and he told me to forgive you. Nickel had told Snicker, "It wasn't just Pop to blame." Nickel had succumbed to Post Traumatic Stress Disorder, pneumonia, and other maladies brought on by his old injuries sustained in Nam.

As Snicker and I talked openly (and with the Vets, our brothers) in front of the Salem Medical Center sharing memories, more facts, certain truths, and legend came to the surface. Apparently the military and especially the Veterans Administration hid the fact that Three Survived. As it turned out, Nickel, Snicker, and I thought all the others were dead (Nickel's and Snicker's paths eventually crossed; they did not know about me). The three of us were scattered abroad and eventually back to the United States.

The VA questioned us many times over the years and they were as perplexed about The Phantom Soldier as we were. We all thought that he helped save our rears (the VA personnel named him Angel). The Marines that came to our rescue denied ever seeing or airlifting such a character.

Our Phantom Angel was a mystery and more than likely would remain a mystery. Snicker told me he thought perhaps The Phantom Soldier was following our unit of thirteen from the beginning (when we left the armory), and that he was reporting to some covert operations command and linked by shortwave radio of some sort with the USS Roosevelt. Snicker said that Nickel had come to the same conclusion as he had. Nickel and Snicker reminisced many times and determined that The Angel had been there. The Roosevelt would never acknowledge our rescue.

Neither Snicker or Nickel had normal family lives, no last known stateside addresses, and had necessarily been transported to different shelters and VA Hospitals based on their conditions (physical and mental needs).

Snicker's once black hair was now gray (Giant Oak Trees Adorned With Spanish Moss), and his huge athletic body was down to about one hundred and fifty pounds from his youthful two hundred and thirty pounds. He was a shadow of the mighty warrior that I knew before our encounter in country in Nam. Snicker told me that the old man with the machete had struck him near his right shoulder causing a deep cut that almost severed his shoulder destroying his clavicle. "It was miraculous that he did not hit my main artery," Snicker said.

Apparently, I had struck the old man a split second to late as he followed through and struck Snicker with a severe blow (Snicker told me he could not have handled the old man). He also told me that he grew to love Nickel like a brother, and that they both decided they would not hate my memory, but love me instead.

Snicker usually talked excitedly (rattling on) complaining about all the years and not being able to grab a decent night's sleep. Free from the repeated nightmares of Nam, all of us at the park bench cried, as Snicker slumped down in the park bench, totally exhausted.

I heard a whimpering, a moan, and sniffling as all of us looked upon Snicker sleeping soundly. One of his humongous severely tattooed Veteran friends picked him up and sat him in his wheelchair. Snicker snored peacefully. That day ended with peace between two men.

Life moved on as I periodically went to the Salem Medical Center in Roanoke for medical checkups. I always visited with Snicker when I went there. We would tell our story each from our own vantage point. During one of my visits, I told Snicker that I had fainted and that I was sorry for doing so. I felt ashamed for causing the fracas and not helping them enough. I told him of my nightmares and my ten nightly visitors, but that he and Nickel were not among my visitors, and we knew why. Both, Nickel and Snicker had lived. Snicker simply chuckled and snorted when I first shared my feelings about my weakness.

After I had visited Snicker several times, he told me that after the attack started I was kicking and hitting everybody, including him, even as I was knocked off my feet onto the hard floor. Soon after he was injured he had fallen on me, and then a severely injured Nickel was tossed on top of both of us. As I listened, my nightmare became a composite from the three of us.

Snicker said respectfully, "You were a crazy man, a Ragin' Cajun (a Raging Cajun). That was the first time I had ever heard the term Raging Cajun. I accepted the term as complimentary, just as Snicker intended it. I had been called a Cajun, but never a Raging Cajun, which I prefer to more flamboyant flagrant insulting names.

The VA never acknowledged our Phantom Angel's existence, a mystery to this day. I told Snicker of my revelation that our Phantom Angel had been Charlie McCarthy, and he accepted my opinion skeptically, but never once questioned my assertion. I never trusted the VA with this concept. Our rescuers documented thirteen male US Military Black Ops Soldiers removed and not fourteen.

Approximately two years after first seeing Snicker at the VA, I was told in a phone call from a Liaison at the VA in Roanoke that Snicker had passed on (he had developed pneumonia and died from old wounds suffered in Nam). I was devastated, but I realized that Snicker now lived peacefully and spiritually with Our Heavenly Father. I regret that I never told Snicker that I loved him, but I did love him. *Je regretted que je n'ai jamais dit que je l'aimais Snickers.*

According to Snicker it was eventually determined, by some well-placed covert sources, that The Brig sent us on the village evacuation mission to get us out of his way while he convinced visitors from The US Army Inspector General's Office (powers that be) that he had once again gained control of the M16 rifles. The Brig alone and no one else had found the misplaced weapons. He told The US Army Inspectors that they could visually see, count, and verify that the one thousand M16 (I specifically witnessed AR15/M16) rifles were in secure stores.

Snicker and Nickel found out through The Grapevine and what they considered reliable sources that their Angel (my Phantom Angel) was possibly a member of The US Army Inspector General's Office (never acknowledged or proven). Possibly the hump on his back had been a radio emitting static sounds; he was following our every move and had for a considerable time been helping in the investigation of a drug cartel run by the very suspicious Brig.

The Brig later disappeared and it was widely believed he worked covertly on both sides and or had crossed over to the Vietcong, eventually disappearing completely. During one of my visits with Snicker he told me a friend had told him that The Brig knew that the villagers we were sent to evacuate were hostile to our US Military, and he sent us on the mission because he wanted to get rid of us.

Not unlike our American Indians placed on reservations, the French speaking Vietnamese Villagers (the old man with the machete spoke mostly French) had been promised and had waited for rations, never getting these provisions. The Villagers determined that the The Brig could not be trusted, and they had become angry. My team and I were not made privy to the hostility that existed between The Old Man and The Brig.

There are many war stories told in huddles outside VA hospital emergency rooms and in city parks by Veterans. Over the years, Snicker had heard many such stories through The Grapevine. One such story, that Snicker believed to be valid, is that the forces that later followed us (our thirteen men) into Vietnam and parts of Cambodia found starving people; people who had been deceived by promises of rations and help (people who had been deceived much like our American Indians on United States reservations).

French speaking fisher people have always survived best and it was evident that most other less capable or lazy people, less self-reliant, had been hooked on opium. It was evident that The Old Man had been dealing opium and other drugs with The Brig and other sinister forces for provisions and protection. Promised provisions and protection were never received.

Many who attacked our small force had believed we were a part of this criminal dark force. A grandson of The Old Man told our rescuing forces the story of what had happened that day (the grandson related an eye witness account). The man said that his Grandfather (The Old

Man) had in fact screamed death in French not English. Morte` in French means death to the murderers of our people. Snicker told me, "We, the thirteen of us, were murderers."

Over the years according to my wife, I have often awoke muttering loudly *maude or morte`*, both French words. Although this had occurred many times over the years, neither Barbara or I had ever recognized or interpreted the grunting guttural sounds or words that had been spoken in French so many years ago in Vietnam. Barbara had not repeated any of the sounds to me except to nudge me and say, "You are grunting, you are making those noises again, roll over and quiet down." "Quiet down," she would say.

The Old Man had been screaming in French and he had been saying the word murder or death (*morte`* in French). One day I related this to Snicker. Snicker said, "Pop, you were probably placed in charge because you could understand and speak French." "Who knew," Snicker added. Snicker said to me, "The word that The Old Man screamed that day was probably French, just as you said, "*La mort*, death, murder. Murderer, *moor dehrrr rh ehr*."

I said to Snicker, "It just wasn't your last day or mine." "It wasn't our turn to die," Snicker replied. "The day or the hour is not ours to know," Snicker said. I thought, "Snicker found God."

Epilogue to: "Three Survived"

In retrospect it was Snicker who lamented with me that he and Nickel had often discussed a legend among the Vietnamese villagers about the Girl and The Brig. The legend had been perpetuated for years by some of The Brig's servants long after we had left Vietnam. This legend included the rumors of the fate of the young girl that we had met in the compound. The young girl was very attached to The Brig.

I suspected that The Brig was not a general, but a lower ranking commissioned officer. This was difficult to prove, because like us, he never wore rank or insignia. We accepted, as fact, that he was placed in charge of the compound and all the inhabitants. We had no reason to question Military authority.

At the compound, I took immediate notice of this very slight in stature young Vietnamese girl. Judging from her flawless skin and very youthful fluid movements, I had thought her to be about twelve years of age. This young girl had wavy raven black hair and had the name Girl. She wore grayish brown long pajamas which struck well below her ankles. Girl was very subservient to The Brig. She fetched his coffee, shirts, boots, slippers and all of his meals. Girl always drank from The Brig's cup or glass and ate from his plate before she served him or before she ate herself.

The Grapevine at the military compound informed my team that all meals were prepared at The Girl's direction. Vietnamese, Cambodian or Chinese servants prepared the meals. These people set the tables, made the beds and cleaned the buildings. They also washed, ironed and folded The Brig's clothes. These servants offered to perform the same duties for our thirteen member team, but we declined.

While I was in the US Military compound, I witnessed that the young girl hardly spoke and when she did speak it was in The Brig's ear. The Girl spoke in murmurs or whispers, and she always stayed within five or six feet of The Brig. She could not enter The Brig's space unless he gestured to her by word or hand.

The Girl was totally under The Brig's control. I witnessed her fetching his slippers and or boots and putting them on his feet. She also kept his boots clean and highly polished. For all intents and purposes, she appeared to be a slave that owed reverence for and homage to The Brig. The Grapevine rumored that she was being held against her will, but I felt this was not the case. We found out later that The Girl adored The Brig.

The Grapevine rumors further informed me (us) that her Grandfather was a villager of immense prestige who lived some distance away near the North Mekong Delta, very close to North Vietnam. The Girl's grandfather, it was rumored, wanted her returned to him otherwise she would have no name from his family until she returned to her people in the village. Girl (as The Brig called her) was considered dead, and she would live again only after she set foot in her grandfather's domain, no matter her physical condition, or her past with The Brig.

No matter where or when you saw The Brig, the girl would be close by often brandishing a locked and loaded M14 rifle. She watched his every move and even stayed near him at night guarding him while he slept (the girl seemed to sleep little, if any). No one attempted to explain any of the seemingly affectionate attachment that The Girl and The Brig exhibited for each other; there were never any sexual or sensual indications displayed between the two. The Brig never showed any outright affection toward the young girl; none of us ever noticed him touching her. It was quite evident that The Girl worshipped him. She displayed this with her eyes and works.

Legend has it that Girl left with The Brig when he was recalled to the States, but instead he disappeared. Grapevine reported that they left for North Vietnam and then went to Cambodia. Legend has it that the man known as Lochinvar and his young maiden left by way of The South Mekong River in a large white skiff powered by an outboard motor. The skiff had the word Lochinvar stenciled in red on both sides of the bow.

Snicker and I further concluded, during our visits, that we had both encountered Girl's machete wielding grandfather. Snicker and I both concluded that on that fateful bloody day, we were supposed to have returned The Old Man's granddaughter to him. When he saw that she was not with our group, he realized that she was gone from his family forever. As this realization came to his mind, he attacked us.

The horrible anguish of The Old Man is now, after all these years, quite understandable. Upon my further reflection, the warehouse burning reminded me then of Manderley burning and The Fire in Rayne of my youth. I hate fires more than I hate alligators and or crocodiles. The dragons in my nightmares haunt me to this day.

Book of Daniel, Chapter 3, Verses 22 thru 25, King James Version of The Holy Bible

22   Therefore because the king's commandment was urgent, and the furnace exceeding hot, the flames of the fire slew those men that took up Shadrack, Meshack, and Abednego.

23   And these three men, Shadrack, Meshack, and Abednego, fell down bound into the midst of the burning fiery furnace.

24   Then Nebuchadnezzar the king was astonished, and rose up in haste, and spake, and said unto his counselors, Did not we cast three men bound into the midst of the fire? They answered and said unto the king, True, O king.

25   He answered and said, Lo, I see four men loose, walking in the midst of the fire, and they have no hurt; and the form of the fourth is like the Son of God.

The Son of God saved Shadrach, Meshach, and Abednego and he saved us, the three American Black Ops Soldiers who survived, Three Survived. "I always thought there had to be more than this time, this place," Snicker said. When he said this he caused me to think of the possible End of Days spoken of in various books of the Bible (Old and New Testament Books of The King James Version of The Holy Bible).

Book of Genesis, Chapter 26, Verse 3, King James Version (1611) *"Soijourne in this land, and I will be with thee, and I will bless thee, and unto thy seed I will give all these countries, and I will perform the oath, which I sware unto Abraham thy father;"*

"Light"

Defeated in word but not in thought,
my thoughts coupled with desires,
have since seen me thru.
Thru bright of day and dark of night,
my path guided by Noble men of light.

By: Rhone` Sonnier Louviere`, written in 1961

"Lumiere" (Francais)

*Defait en parole mais pas dans la pensee,
mes pensees couple avec des desirs,
ont depuis vu me thru.*

*Thru lumineux de la journee et obscurite de la nuit,
Mon cheminement guide par les hommes nobles de la
lumiere.*

Un poeme par, Rhone` Sonnier Louviere`

UFO Visits Pascagoula
"OVNI Visites Pascagoulal"

On October 10, 1973, fifteen different people including two policemen reported seeing a large, silver UFO flying slowly over a housing project in St. Tammany Parish, New Orleans, Louisiana.

At 9:00 p.m. on the night of October 11, 1973 nineteen year old Calvin Parker and forty-two year old Charles Hickson, both from Gautier, Mississippi, saw a silver metallic object that they became convinced was an alien spacecraft. (Someone else, not these two men, later would say that it was an Unidentified Flying Object.)

Parker and Hickson were fishing on the banks of the Pascagoula River when they suddenly heard a buzzing sound behind them. They turned toward the sound and noted that the buzzing came from a glowing object with blue lights. The object was hovering a few feet above the ground about thirty feet from the bank of the river. The two men reported being taken aboard the ship by beings that were about five feet tall with bullet shaped slits for eyes. The men claimed that after being taken on board the ship, they were placed in separate compartments and examined by the beings.

Both Parker and Hickson passed lie detector tests. The men that handled their testing said that they believed Parker and Hickson, but could provide no plausible explanation for their information being truthful. The final technical assertion of their testing was that the men were telling the truth.

Most people do not believe that there is other life in the universe; most people believe that we are the only planet with human life. I have always believed that the two men saw something, but I cannot explain all of what they may have seen. I want to believe Parker and Hickson because of the events in New Orleans, Louisiana on October 10,

1973. After Vietnam, no one seemed to believe Nickel, Snicker, or me concerning our Phantom Angel; no one believed that Parker and Hickson had a UFO encounter in Pascagoula, Mississippi (near the grain elevator on the west bank of the Pascagoula, River). I never doubted the men's sincerity, just their reliability. "After all, God did create all things," I thought.

There was then and continues to be great skepticism about this encounter with a UFO. The two men admitted that they had been drinking and claimed to have had a brief encounter (abduction and examination) with/by aliens (much like Randy Quaid's character in the movie "Independence Day" written and produced in 1996 by Dean Devlin and directed by Roland Emmrich). The night of Parker and Hickson's alleged UFO sighting visibility was great, the stars were bright, and the sky was clear.

During the time period of the Parker/Hickson sighting, I worked at Ingalls Shipbuilding (Litton Industries) not far from the grain elevator. Along with a partner, usually a young man named Sweatman, I traveled all over the west bank shipyard. We most often visited Destroyers that were nearing completion and shipment to Iran. (During our circuits, we would often wander around talking with inspectors, or I would visit Carl Simmons, a Shipfitter Leadman and my father-in-law).

Parker and Hickson were not criminal types. They had no record of any offenses and were reported to be good family men. At the time to discount their sighting much was made of their drinking habits and that what they saw was in the bottom of a whiskey bottle. To this day I am empathetic with the two common men, though given to drink, who witnessed and or had an Unidentified Flying Object encounter beside the Pascagoula River.

On the night of the encounter, Sweatman and I made our nightly circuits while performing our jobs as Quality Inspectors. We were standing topside one of the Landing Helicopter Assault Ships being built by Ingalls (West Bank Facility). We had an unobstructed view, from over one hundred feet in the air, and I did look in the direction of the Pascagoula River Bridge and the grain elevator. These two men had some kind of encounter, no doubt, and whatever they encountered would have been visible to me from my vantage point on top of the LHA. What they saw from their vantage point by the grain elevator, I don't know, we just have their account (I saw nothing).

Knowing what happened to Parker and Hickson is one reason I can have patience with the VA Hospital and their psychologists for not believing the Phantom Angel part of Three Survived. Nickel, Snicker and I told our stories from the same vantage point but there are differences. Over the many years as we told our story to many people, we (Nickel, Snicker and I) agreed that the Phantom Angel was in fact there and helped the Creatures save our lives.

The major difference between Three Survived and the UFO encounter is that we were quite sober and an elite professional military unit. I repeat once more that we were well trained and ready, but we could not lock and load or fire our weapons until a life was in eminent danger, and we had warned the opposition several times. This was a heavy and awesome responsibility.

When Nickel, Snicker, and I had heard the rumbling, thunderous sounds above and approaching the monstrous warehouse, and we jointly witnessed the lights coming from the heavens, we thought our very world was coming to an end. We were terrified beyond comprehension; we all three soiled our fatigues. My initial thoughts when I heard the sounds and saw the lights was that we were going to experience an alien UFO encounter; an experience we would not live through.

179

When I first heard and read of the UFO encounter by Parker and Hickson I thought it to be humorous. The two blue collar workers had experienced an Unidentified Flying Object encounter, and we three survivors in military uniforms in Vietnam had perhaps experienced a Heavenly Body, a Phantom Angel.

The rest of the UFO story was never made public. Just across the Pascagoula River from where Parker and Hickson had been on the night of October 11, 1973, there were three nuclear fast attack submarines being built (the submarines were dockside). The river is about five football fields (500 yards) in width at this point. The City of Pascagoula begins about another two hundred yards (200 yards) from that side of the river.

I worked second shift at Ingalls Nuclear Shipbuilding East Bank Facility for several years, from 1967 to 1970, and later I worked at the West Bank Facility until 1978. Several times while I worked the docks on boats (submarines) I had witnessed strange, but explainable phenomena involving water and reflections caused by light and salt (brine water).

The building of submarines would start with a single beveled curved steel plate approximately three inches thick and twelve feet by twelve feet. The steel plate was beveled for later welding. The steel plate was laid in a specific location and at a designated pitch, declivity angle of fifteen degrees, on a dock specially prepared and fabricated to the tightest of tolerances. These preparations were for launching the submarine after completion.

The submarine was nested and held in the air by support legs and cross beams like those used when building merchant ships or sailboats. Each submarine was completed to certain specifications and painted numerous times with orange rust preventive paint, sanded then repainted again, many times. Inspectors checked all

180

building procedures and specifications ascertaining that the submarine was being built properly. The boat was completed internally to a determined stage, painted black and verified for stern launch into the Pascagoula, River, after which it was taken by tug boats to a water dock for further completion.

At the stage just before launch, I had on several occasions witnessed a visual phenomenon caused by the light from the shipyard and salt water. The combination of shipyard lights and slightly choppy salt water projected images across the Pascagoula River onto the sides of the large grain elevator and shore line on the opposite west bank. (The projected giant image reminded me of the Batman symbol used in movies. The Batman symbol is projected in the sky and onto buildings.)

There were many lighted buildings behind the submarines. The buildings were used by US Navy support staff during the construction of the vessels. There were also numerous lighted material warehouses lining every dock and road. The point is, there were many lights and many diverse shapes were cast onto the west bank of the river.

During a full moon accompanied by slightly choppy waves and a multitude of various lights on the east bank of the river, I witnessed a reflection of gleaming light cast onto the white grain elevator and bank across the river. I witnessed this phenomenon while standing topside of the Puffer and then the Aspro Submarines. The choppy illumination was beautiful, and I could instantly tell it was a reflection, as from a mirror, of east bank lights projected onto the white wall of the grain elevator. The reflection appeared to be a shimmering waving flag of yellow highlights in various hues as that of a rainbow.

My opinion of the Unidentified Flying Object, UFO sighting, and not the boarding or physical examinations, was then and is now that possibly their discernment and illumination (understanding, comprehension) of The Book of Ezekiel, Chapter 1 (King James Version of The Holy Bible) prepared the two men to be susceptible to visions of a vessel, apparition, and accompanying alien beings. I read in various newspaper articles that the two men had been attending religious revivals and studying The Book of Ezekiel the week before their encounter. Alcohol became a potent catalyst to their minds rendering their thoughts even more susceptible.

Book of Ezekiel, Chapter 1, Verses 1-28 (condensed), King James Version of The Holy Bible *And I looked, and, behold, a whirlwind came out of the north, a great cloud, and a fire infolding itself, and a brightness was about it, and out of the midst thereof as the colour of amber, out of the midst of the fire (v-4); Sole of their feet sparkles, colour of burnished brass (v-7); like burning coals of fire, appearance of lamps, fire was bright, went forth lightning (v-14); appearance of a flash of lightning (v-16); wheels and their work, colour of a beryl (v-22); firmament upon the heads, colour of amber, appearance of fire round about within it, his loins upward, downward, appearance of fire, brightness round about; bow (rainbow), cloud in the day of rain, appearance of the brightness round about, appearance of the likeness of the glory of the LORD (v-28).*

(Note: Companion Reference Bible and Strong's Concordance, Ezekiel 1:4 Old Testament, Amber - Hebrew, chashmal (khashman') bronze or polished spectrum metal. Whirlwind – Hebrew, ruwach (roo' - akh) by resemblance breath, or even violent exhalation.)

The illumination from the east bank reflected off the white grain elevator into a mist that usually hung over the Pascagoula River on warm nights (the mist caused by cool water and warm air). The reflection was again cast back over to the west bank onto the high marsh grass adjacent and beside the grain elevator and onto a slight hill running up from the river to the roads leading to and from Ingalls Shipbuilding, Litton Industries, West Bank Facility.

The UFO was the projected image of the submarine on stilts or legs, the launch pad, from across the way giving the impression of a silhouette or some kind of egg or saucer shaped vessel already prepared for in the inebriated minds of Parker and Hickson.

I thought, "There must be more than this, something somewhere, somehow more than this, and then I knew, I am not alone."

Barbara and the Sierra Madre Mountains

My favorite excursions have always been those experienced with my wife Barbara and I have always relished these times together. I have traveled to Asia, Europe, The former Soviet Union, The Middle East, Latin America, and South America for the military, business and pleasure. My most enjoyable sojourn has been with my wife and soulmate Barbara to Monterrey, Mexico. While I was there on business, we took a guided trek by horseback into The Sierra Madre Mountains.

In 1988, I traveled as a Corporate Quality Manager, acting as a Global Supplier Quality Engineer Representative for a premier bathroom brass fixtures manufacturing company. My assignment was to analyze and report on the culture relative to cultural effects on Supply Side Management, in particular as regarded trucking our products and materials back and forth across The United States and Mexico border. This report would be included as part of an extensive supplier survey which I was to conduct and prepare for our corporation's president. My passport and travel visas, not required in Mexico, always indicated that I was a tri-lingual Spanish, French, and English Teacher/Professor traveling on business and for pleasure.

It was in more of a teaching capacity, on this particular trip, that I decided to pay my wife's airfare and take her along with me. Our host supplier company representatives had previously met Barbara and been entertained at our home in both Dallas, Texas and later in Abilene, Texas. I worked in Abilene and also attended Abilene Christian University.

I loved Barbara's companionship as we talked and talked during our flight from Abilene to Dallas/Fort Worth, Texas and onto Monterrey, Mexico.

During the first few days in Monterrey, while I worked, Barbara browsed the Mexican markets and walked in the many beautiful large and small parks. On one particular day, Barbara traveled by bus into the Sierra Madre Mountains for a short trip to a popular waterfall. While on the tour bus, accompanied by all Mexican occupants, Barbara joyfully sang along with them as they sang Doris Day's "Que Sera Sera."

Barbara found the people of Mexico to be very happy and spontaneous, singing and taking pictures. While on her walk about with the Mexican people, Barbara was asked about her husband, she told them that I was French. They asked her if her husband had blue eyes and she told them that he had hazel blue eyes. The bus driver related that there were blue eyed Mexicans in the area where they currently were, and that they were the result of French occupation of the area. The assimilation of Mexican (Spanish) and French was and continues to be indicative of eventual peaceful coexistence of diverse cultures.

Each evening after work, Barbara and I would walk, talk, sit and watch locals in the city parks. We observed the very romantic and demonstrative Latin lovers on the park benches. We most particularly enjoyed viewing and studying the beautiful bronze statues that had turned hues of green. Most of these statues were water features, beautiful and peaceful. Most days there was entertainment on gazebos in the parks lively Mexican music and lively dancing. We most particularly enjoyed the guitar serenades.

In the middle of all this festivity and happiness, as we were walking back to our hotel, we witnessed a barefoot child wearing a flimsy short sleeved cotton dress lying on the concrete at the entrance to a department store in Monterrey proper. In broken Spanish I managed to ask her, "Why are you lying in the doorway, isn't the concrete cold?" The girl replied, "I am not cold, my Mother is inside working in this store; she will be off in two hours.

I am waiting to walk my Mother home; I want to be sure she arrives home safely. The streets can be dangerous at night."

The graciousness and loving dedication of this particular child to her mother is representative of all the Mexican people's love of family. I have witnessed that the Mexican people are very family oriented. This little child's love for her mother touched the very core of my soul.

I have never forgotten this incident that Barbara and I witnessed together, just as I will never forget all the poverty that I have witnessed around the world (various locations, different countries). I have witnessed some of the worst poverty and deprivation in our own country, The Appalachian Mountains in the United States of America. We help people all over the world and expend so little effort and money assisting the Appalachian people in coal mining country.

Barbara had talked a lot about her tour to the waterfall in The Sierra Madre, the treacherous Sierra Madre Mountains. She told me that she had ridden to the top of the waterfall in a donkey drawn cart but that there were guided horse rides available. She asked me, "Wouldn't it be fun to ride a horse in the Sierra Madre?"

(I remembered that these mountains are depicted as extremely hazardous in the 1948 American film "The Treasure of the Sierra Madre," starring Humphrey Bogart, written and directed by John Huston also starring Walter Huston, the director's father. This is a Hollywood adaptation of the novel by the same name written by B. Traven. The movie characters were in the mountains to prospect for gold.)

With memories of this film, and some trepidation, Barbara and I scheduled a Sunday tour and started our adventure. Our tour stopped at a jewelry store, then in a small town for lunch in a purely authentic Mexican restaurant and a tour of an old Catholic Church, and onto the waterfall adventure. We were having great fun, we both love history and ambience.

After arriving at the waterfall check in location, we told them we wanted to take the horse tour. I was mounted on a small horse named Napoleon and Barbara's horse was named Josephine. I sang under my breath and whistled to Napoleon (I had previously ridden horses in the mountains of South America. Some places that I visited could only be reached by horse). As I sang to my horse, (I must interject that I do not have the singing abilities of my cousin, Jo`El Sonnier) Napoleon turned his ears and snorted in appreciation or displeasure, I did not know which.

Our guides led us over treacherous mountain paths. Our horses walked very close to the edge of precipices; we were told not to look down. I was very scared, but observed and felt certain, with some amusement, that it hardly bothered Barbara (she has always loved horses, she was in Horsey Heaven). Barbara seemed quite comfortable in the saddle and as usual totally in charge.

We reached the top of the mountain where the waterfall spilled down, it was beautiful. We made it through the experience better informed, unharmed, and we returned to Dallas, Texas and our busy schedules.

Assimilation of the French along with other cultures has occurred throughout the world, sometimes not peacefully. Whether peaceably or by forceful occupation, the French have had and continue to contribute to the societies they migrate to and assimilate into. First and foremost, I am a Christian American, secondly a Mississippian, thirdly a Biloxian, fourth a Frenchman, and there is no fifth.

Singapore/Indonesia

Indonesia, officially the Republic of Indonesia, is a country in Southeast Asia and Oceania. Indonesia is an archipelago comprising approximately 17,508 islands. The first principle of Indonesia's philosophical foundation is Pancasila. (Pancasila is belief in the one and only God.) A number of different religions are practiced in Indonesia, and their collective influence on the country's political, economic and cultural life is significant.

The Indonesian Constitution guarantees freedom of religion. However, the government only recognizes six official religions. Those recognized religions are Islam, Protestantism, Catholicism, Hinduism, Buddhism and Confucianism. Indonesian law requires that every Indonesian citizen hold an identity card that identifies that person with one of these six religions. Indonesia does not recognize agnosticism or atheism, and blasphemy is illegal.

In the 2010 Indonesian census, 87.18% of Indonesians identified themselves as Muslim (predominantly Sunnis, also includes Shias and Armadas), 6.96% Protestant, and 1.3% Catholic. With many different religions practiced in Indonesia conflicts between followers of different religions arise periodically. Moreover, Indonesia's political leadership has played an important role in the relations between groups, both positively and negatively, including the Transmigration Program, which has caused a number of conflicts in the eastern region of the country.

I was Director of Quality Assurance for Candle Corporation of America from 1999-2002. At that time, Candle Corp was a major competitor of Yankee Candle Corporation. Candle Corporation of America at that time was seeking to cost reduce its glass jar cost by moving much of its supplier base to Indonesia. I was called upon to travel to Indonesia, near Sumatra, and perform a supplier evaluation. I was to perform certain scientific and quality testing of the glass and measurements of paraffin in the candles and sand in the glass according to procedures provided. Sand islands are in abundance in this region, and the sand is actually siphoned from some islands as the islands rise and the sand islands disappear as the siphoning is completed.

My travel plans required me to begin in Winston-Salem, North Carolina and travel to Singapore where I would meet a traveling companion. The Frenchman, as he was called, was a bilingual escort of unusual mental and physical talents, and he knew his way around the islands and straights.

On arriving in Singapore, I was greeted by an American, The Frenchman. This gentleman had exceptional engineering and language capability (I will not describe his stature are ethnicity) who was to serve as my personal driver, interpreter, and negotiator. This young multi-lingual man, in addition to having an outstanding education, was an Attorney-at-Law and understood, as well as, spoke fluent Mandarin Chinese. His family consisted of a wife from Thailand and three young daughters. His family lived with their Grandmother in Thailand (he had another home in Kuala Lumpur).

The glass company that I was to visit had their chauffeur pick us up at the small airport in Sumatra to take us directly to the glass company. The chauffeur told us, "The owner calls me Driver, you must do the same, it is best." When we reached the glass company, the driver (the driver was a Chinese man who served as personal chauffeur and security for the company president) eased the car to the gate and began pulling forward. There were ten masked armed men on dirt bikes blocking our path.

The driver said to us, "Don't worry about them, there is no danger here. The bikers (with motorized bikes) aggressively support the Blind Cleric." "They will part and let us through, they recognize the owner's personal car," the driver continued. The driver told us, "The owner of the glass company is Chinese, and he speaks Mandarin (I could speak a little at the time), most owners of companies in Indonesia, about seventy-five percent, are Chinese."

Suddenly the bikers parted and we drove through the gate into the front parking area and from there we were taken to the front entrance. The owner of the glass company was waiting outside the front door; he greeted us enthusiastically and shook our hands firmly. "Welcome to my company and to Indonesia, let us move inside where you can be more comfortable and we can serve tea," he said.

I could only see one entrance to the glass company, and there was a guard shack at either side of it. The security guards were dressed in black police military fatigues, military gear, and carried weapons. Their military counterparts were dressed in camouflaged military fatigues and they had on more impressive gear and weapons. The military wore various types of berets in different colors; they were quite impressive and looked very fit and well trained, nevertheless I still did not feel safe.

A brief meeting was held with the owner, and we discussed our plans for the next seven days. Afterwards we all walked through the main gate (we were flanked by security) and through the armed bikers who now wore their own style of red beret.

Our little group made its way to the Sales Outlet across the street from the glass company. We were given a complete tour of the Sales Outlet and company personnel made presentations describing products that our Sales Representative might be interested in. We could look through the front glass door and windows and see what was going on across the road at the front gate. There were now more bikers than before, and they were in constant motion so I could not count their number. I was extremely excited and scared. We decided to leave the Sales Outlet through the side door which led into an alley thereby avoiding possible sighting and confrontation with the armed bikers. The Candle Corp Sales Rep was scared, hell I was scared, I thought.

The Candle Corp Sales Representative said to me, "I have been told by some very reliable friends that you were in the military, is that right?" he asked. I replied, "That is correct, you can rely on me." He asked me, "Can you get us out of here?" I told the Sales Rep, "I can, but you must leave your camera for safe keeping with these friends in this building."

I coached the Sales Rep, "Let's walk down this alley to the back of this building to the driver of the owner's car. Let's walk away quietly, hands by our sides with our palms to the front, do not stop. Keep your hands away from your pockets, and let's just walk away calmly."

We did walk away and got into the waiting car, and the driver drove us out of the city proper to a more certain safety. The driver drove us to a resort in the mountains of Sumatra, and we stayed in a five star hotel for the three day weekend at the owner's embarrassed, expense. This precaution was for our safety. When the owner felt it was safe we returned to the city.

After several days at the glass manufacturing site performing our assigned tasks, we were met by a Vice President of Sales and Marketing. The representative of Candle Corp had red hair, a ruddy complexion (possibly an Irishman), was small in stature and very feminine (which was of no concern to me) and apprehensive of the political climate.

After the Sales and Marketing Rep came, we were taken to the jungle to meet with some of the militants to discover the culture and whether or not we could do

191

business. We saw things we should not have seen. Our security hunted and provided miniature pigs which were roasted on rotisserie spit rods over an open fire. While sitting by the fire the militants that were talking to the owner told him that they in fact were not in support of the Blind Cleric. Despite public display some militants were talking covertly about peacefully removing him from power.

Three calm uneventful days later we left Indonesia and started our return home. The owner and the Indonesian Government, as well as the government of Singapore, had sent us to the resort in the mountains for their own political reasons and our safety.

On my return to Elkin, North Carolina and Candle Corp, I reported what seemed to be terrorist sympathizers at the manufacturing facility and in the outskirts of the city proper (jungle). Candle Corp executives did not want a written report. They did not want to discuss any of the details of my trip; they wanted me to shut up; and they wanted what I had seen and heard to go away, period!!!

I told Candle Corp executives emphatically, "I will never return to Indonesia or Singapore for this company again, never again, never ever again." A few days or weeks later 9/11 happened, the United States was attacked by terrorists.

I did not return to Indonesia, but Candle Corp attempted to send Terry H, the Manufacturing Plant Quality Manager, on September 11, 2001. I remember relating my story about conditions in Indonesia to Terry and telling him not to make the trip. "I do not feel right about it," I said. Terry H's plane was turned back on the runway at the Winston Salem, North Carolina Airport. The Twin Towers in Manhattan had been attacked by terrorists (9/11). At that same time The Frenchman, my Indonesian escort, had disappeared for his own protection. The Vice President of The United States, Dick Chaney, had grounded all flights and ordered all US Airports closed until he ordered otherwise.

On my return trip to the United States from Indonesia, I recall that I was not allowed any back tracking. I was to have, as near as possible, the same plans (route) as I had taken to Singapore and Indonesia with special care given to no detours or surprises.

On my return trip, I had to sleep in a cubicle at the Singapore Airport. I had a nightmare about Big Harry. I had heard the Indians say, "Be careful when you visit the outer islands." "What in the world are they talking about?" I asked my escort, The Frenchman. (For clarification, The Frenchman was my Indonesian escort/partner, not Driver, not me the Cajun Frenchman, as I am sometimes called.)

The Frenchman told me that the Indians tell tales about something humongous out there on one of the islands. They are horrified at what it is and will not travel in past the beach when they work on the islands. In my nightmare, I find myself looking at the Indians who are in fear, and I look past the sandy beach into the jungle and see nothing special.

The Indians shout hysterically, some in French some in Chinese, "He has come, he has come. It is Big Harry!" *Il est venu, il est Big Harry ils ont crié hystériquement.* "It is Big Harry," they shout over and over, as frantically they run for the boats, get on board and quickly head out into the ocean leaving me standing in shock on the beach.

I am experiencing a nightmare. "This is not good, not good at all," I say to myself. In my dream I see a deep hole up ahead of me, the hole is perhaps fifty feet from me, and I see another hole closer, about thirty feet from me. The holes are big and deep, possibly 12 feet square by six feet deep. I am horrified and start to turn and run, but my body will not respond fast enough to follow the message from my brain.

Some big thing, that I cannot see, is making giant steps and holes in the sandy beach and is coming at me and gripping me in its fist. At this point, I felt long hair. I realized that the Indians had been shouting Big Hairy, not Big Harry. I woke up suddenly, gasping for air, safe in my sleeping cubicle at the Singapore Airport. *"Big Poilu," et non "Big Harry," et j`ai ete tout d`un coup a bout de souffle, et je me suis soudainement eveille.* I looked at the clock and saw that I had three hours before boarding time for my flight home.

(Officially the Republic of Singapore is a Southeast Asian city/state off the southern tip of the Malay Peninsula, one hundred thirty seven kilometers (85 miles) north of the equator. Singapore is an island country made up of sixty-three islands; it is separated from Malaysia by the Straits of Johor to its north and from Indonesia's Riau Islands by the Singapore Strait to the south. Singapore is highly urbanized with very little primary rainforest remaining.)

The Cane
"La Canne"

I always tell my students that The Cane is a prop for walking and telling my story, Three Survived. *Jed is toujours aux etudiants, La Canne, est un accessoire pour la marche et la narration Trois ont survecu.*

In addition to the injuries I suffered to my lower back and legs while being saved in Nam, I would sprain both ankles two years later. I sprained my left ankle in 1964 and my right ankle in 1965. I sprained my ankles while engaged in separate military maneuvers during my return to Delohnega, Georgia. I was acting as an aggressor and advisor to US Army Officers Candidate School (OCS).

It would take some years, as I aged, for these injuries to gradually worsen and then set in and become arthritic leaving me with a slower body and pain in the ankle joints and bottoms of my feet, especially my heels. Use of The Cane as a prop helps me make it through the most arduous longer work and or teaching days. *L'utilisation de "La Canne" comme un accessoire m'aide a le faire a travers le travail le plus ardu lus jour.*

Assimilation (anecdotal)

"Peaceful Conflict Resolutions"

Respect the right to disagree

Express your real concerns

Share common goals

Open yourself to different points of view

Listen carefully to all proposals

Understand the major issues involved

Think about possible consequences

Imagine several possible alternative solutions

Offer some reasonable compromises

Negotiate mutually fair cooperative agreements

Robert E. Valette
1927 – 2008
Wonderful (merveilleux)
Educator, Author, and Creator of humanistic motivational
posters

Second Book of Thessalonians, Chapter 3, Verse 6, 1611
Holy Bible *Now we command you, brethren, in the Name
of our Lord Jesus Christ, that ye withdraw yourselues
from euery Brother that walketh disorderly, and not after
the tradition which hee receiued of vs.*

Second Book of Thessalonians, Chapter 3, Verse 6, KJV
Now we command you, brethren, in the name of our Lord Jesus Christ, that ye withdraw yourselves from every Brother that walketh disorderly, and not after the tradition which he received of us.

Acadians brought solidarity with them to Louisiana, Mississippi, Texas, Alabama, and to every other land they would settle. As one of the first groups to cross the Atlantic and adopt a new identity, Acadians felt connected to each other by their common experiences. They had differences in their backgrounds which would separate the Acadian Cajuns from those who were more established Americans. Acadian Cajuns were not and are not immigrants.

As of 1976, Cajuns were acknowledged as established Americans and recognized as a legal minority culture. By the 1980's ethnicities first marginalized by the American mainstream became valuable as regional flavors. Acadian Cajuns are proud of the place that their work, music, and food occupy in mainstream America.

"Diversity"

Different

Individuals

Valuing

Each other

Regardless of

Skin

Intellect

Talents

Years

By: Author Unknown

Enforce Existing Laws

While I was not sure in the 1960's of the course of action to be taken, I did know that my own knowledge of education and desegregation of all public schools and colleges would help provide an avenue to equal education rights under the law. My plan then was to improve myself and my family while pursuing improvements through fair and reasonable enforcement of active laws pertaining to equal representation of the laws in our public education institutions.

I believed then, as I believe today, that race may play a minor part and not a significant one in the recruitment and placement of students in alignment with a legally pre-approved measurement. I knew then that I must find a path, and that, that path should be through Texas. I believe that path is through legislation that already exists, Separate but Equal, and must be enforced or must be changed in the courts.

We must first enforce existing laws. Existing laws can be elusive and or outright unavailable to average citizens unless they happen to be in the right place, at the right time, performing research to unveil information about a particular condition that may have law applied. While delving into my fantasy to attend college again and write my dissertation, I found information on a Supreme Court Decision which directly applies to Cajuns, meaning me, *moi*, my Cajun relatives and my Cajun friends.

During one of my infrequent phone calls to my brother Mervin (Joe) Sonnier and following some brief exchanges about Daddy's health and Joe's health; I maneuvered our conversation to the original intent of my call. I asked him a leading question, "Joe, do you know that you are a minority?" Joe replied with, "No, I don't know that I am a minority, why do you ask?" To which I responded, "Don't you think you should know if you are in fact a minority." Joe then said, "Okay, now that you have my attention, what is the catch, is this some kind of lead into a Cajun joke?" I said, "No." I think perhaps he expected a punch line of some kind.

Joe went on to say, "Yes, I do think I should know if I am a minority, now tell me exactly what this is about?" I responded to Joe's query with, "There is a 1976 Supreme Court ruling that gave minority status to Cajun Americans." To this Joe said, "I didn't know that. What difference does it make?"

I responded by adding, "You retired a couple of times, first from the Navy and then from teaching college. You applied for jobs with Ingalls Shipbuilding (located on the Pascagoula River, same place there was an alleged UFO sighting and abduction) as an Instructor, but you were never hired." I continued, "You should also have been able to claim minority status at Keesler, along with your veteran retired Navy status, and that probably would have assured more consideration and employment opportunities at Keesler."

We continued our telephone conversation, talking about Daddy's years as a Civil Service worker at Keesler Air Force Base in Biloxi. Daddy received seventy percent of his base pay when he retired after working for thirty years as a Roofer/Carpenter. The conversation about our Daddy's and Mama's lives as Cajun Americans drifted back to having certain rights as complete natural American citizens and what that really means. We explored how a minority status could have helped Daddy with possibly better opportunities for advancement. Daddy retired years before the 1976 ruling. This topic took us back to the main topic, Cajuns as a minority class. I said, "The problem is Cajun is not on the list of fifteen or twenty minorities such as American Indian, Eskimo, Hispanic (not of European descent) and the correct classification of Cajun is white French Caucasian of European descent. The US Government's list of minorities is extensive, but Cajun is not on any list of minorities, unless you consider other (explain). At least the other category can be used."

I reminded Joe that in 1976 I was an employee at Ingalls. I had been there since 1967, and I was happy with my employment. I had a Secret Clearance, and I was working on fast attack nuclear submarines such as the Aspro and the Puffer. After discharge from the US Army and working some minor jobs, I was introduced to and entered an Apprentice Pipefitter Program eventually going to work at Ingalls as a pipefitter and progressed to different jobs through self-improvement. I was a Senior Submarine Quality Systems Test Engineer when I left Ingalls in 1978. I was not at any point informed by anyone that I was a minority then or ever (now).

Furthermore, I said to Joe, "I did not seek any special treatment or contemplate being considered more equal, and or separate, but equal, to or from any other person or ethnicity." I asked Joe, "If I had not read about this 1976 Supreme Court Ruling, how would either of us know anything about it today?"

Joe asked, "Ronnie, what point are you making?" I replied, "If the minority status is not sufficiently publicized to reach all people who are Cajun, how can Cajun citizens know and or claim their legal rights." I had lost my brother's interest and attention, and our conversation moved onto family again, and ended with the usual I love you Bro (Ron to Joe) and I love you too Bro (Joe to Ron). We each said, "Bye" and hung up.

Going deeply into contemplation and or my own critical thinking mode, I realized that my conversation with my brother had just led me once more to some deep revelations about fairness and or appeasement. Fairness and or appeasement has been going on for so long that it is shaking the very foundation of our nation and The Constitution of The United States of America, The Declaration of Independence, Our Pledge of Allegiance to

201

the Flag, Our Preamble, The Articles of Confederation, and The Federalist Papers (those notes and letters from our Founding Fathers which left us a message based on core beliefs as borrowed with reverence from The King James Bible, the Word of God from the Manuscripts written I believe by Divine Intervention from Almighty God). These Truths Remain Self Evident, and we are endowed by our Creator with certain inalienable rights…….

However, much as they may have been well intended, back in the 1960's in Biloxi, Reverend John Isgood's and Dr. Mason's actions sought to explore their own personal rights, but they were also protesting unfairness which caused unrest.

I believe the wade-ins on Biloxi Beach led by Isgood and Mason, were for their own self-interests and that of The NAACP (the mission of the National Association for the Advancement of Colored People is to ensure the political, educational, social and economic equality of rights of…..).

I am wading in now, as a minority, a Cajun, and state that it is my opinion Affirmative Action, Separate but Equal, and The Equal Rights Amendment all apply to the same so-called fairness for the poor disadvantaged (disenfranchised) people and is in and of itself discrimination and causes racial strife and divisiveness.

To me, this is a way of spreading the wealth from those who have to those who supposedly have not, until those who have become those who had and now join with the ranks of those who are in fact really poor disadvantaged and become the disenfranchised. This in and of itself is perpetuating discrimination between diverse ethnicities and cultures to lower us all to a state of inequality, a third world nation, taking us backwards to Kings, Queens, and Monarchies.

This is not what we want our leaders to secure on our behalf. I want every American Citizen to have the opportunity to have their own free experiences just as I have had with dogs, alligators, teachers, church, school, work, play, war, family, travel, mistakes, corrections, and brotherhood, but not at another person's expense. If you want and or need something, get your butt out there and earn it! Build that! Yes, you can build that!

Cajuns must enter into and stay grounded in the American mainstream, and not expect favored status whether awarded or not by the state. We are Americans, not Cajun Americans. We are Americans first and Cajuns second, and we are all one. We are not lost; God knows every hair on our heads so how can he not know who we are and what we deserve. We are the ones confused, not our God.

We are the ones who are confused with man's laws, because we do not adhere to our Preamble to The United States Constitution. I contend that our Preamble was written by the Hand of God, and we have to decide that prayer provides answers from God to all our concerns, provided we humble ourselves before him without arrogance and or challenge.

Precedence is a word and action used and practiced by our courts. Our courts may decide to intervene in matters of states' rights verses rights endowed by Our Creator, considering that which may be fair, more than fair in decision making, no discernment involved while leaving God out of the equation. This process of precedence sets the premise of our constitution aside to satisfy authoritarianism.

We are once again in the political isms: socialism, communism, atheism, etcetera et al. *Nous sommes a nouveau dans la politique de l'ISM, le socialisme, le communisme, l'aheisme et cetera et al.*

I say that a white woman in Texas (be she Irish, Cajun, Italian, English, Polish and or any other nationality) has a right (deserves equal and not unequal consideration) to her place in an Austin, Texas University (The University of Texas) as any other male or female of any other ethnicity (more especially a black, African American whose race may have some moderate consideration for the same place, a seat in a class), and this must be based solely on credentials (not on the color of one's skin), and not allowing being black to weigh excessively in consideration by a duly appointed University approving panel.

This University panel must act fairly and judiciously not based on precedence, but on truth and conviction. The decision of The University of Texas and The United States Supreme Court must consider life altering implications of their decision as the decision may affect all of American's higher education institutions, both public and private. Inclusion rather than thoughts and actions of exclusion should be of paramount consideration in rendering a decision soon to take place in early 2013.

My brother Joe, like myself, never considered minority status (no matter the travails of our lives, Joe's on the USS Randolph in the Gulf of Mexico near Cuba, or mine in Vietnam and Germany) as a way of gaining some kind of edge over others, and we continue to feel we need not request any handout (just get the hell out of our way). We are Cajuns who can and will secure our own future.

Through our military service we and our relatives, of diverse cultures, have earned some consideration, but we will not beg for any consideration as an advantage over others. We are not Slaves or Sharecroppers in Indentured Servitude. That is in the past. We are no longer those that were forced into various forms of Indentured Servitude (paid with script or tokens) as were our Irish and other relatives, born into the coal mines of West Virginia (in bondage where there were row houses, shanty shacks, camps without heat or clean running water).

Cajuns are for an indisputable fact not descendants of the mythical Evangeline, but for a fact historically (and biblically) proven to be of The House of Israel, of the ten northern tribes that crossed the Caucasus Mountains, settled Europe (England, Scotland, Ireland, etc.), and came to the Americas and settled. We are of Jacob, renamed by God, Israel. We are French Acadian Cajuns; we are God's children; we are of The House of Israel. God set us free not Lincoln.

I believe that Affirmative Action has outlived its usefulness, if it ever had one, and must go away quietly along with its advocates and lobbyists. Separate but Equal has outlived its original intended purpose, if it had a legitimate purpose, and must go away quietly along with its advocates and lobbyists.

There is need for a thesis and or dissertation from a qualified educator and Cajun who relinquishes his rights to special treatment for past wrongs. I relinquish any rights to special treatment and expect the same from fellow Americans.

I offer my explanation of my childhood and manhood, and submit in this my literary work a mock synopsis of my dissertation.

Separate but Equal, The Law Must Be Enforced

Mock Synopsis of a Dissertation
"Séparés mais égaux"

I dared to dream that one day I would walk the grounds and halls of Abilene Christian University and earn my Master's Degree in Education Supervision. A fantasy, I suppose, but a fantasy that was achievable with the right plan. A goal had to be set and certain short term achievable objectives and a long term commitment to consistent hard work and study.

I had to find the money, convince others that I was worth their investment. Their investment must meet their personal or business requirements and not just my personal ambitions. Completing a rigid course of study and curriculum as well as maintaining above a 3.5 grade point average would be required. I would also have to complete a thesis or extra courses, I did both.

My dream and next plan or goal is to earn a doctorate from Duke University which will require approval of my dissertation and a published work recognized by Duke in Political Science/Public Policy (Sociology). This dissertation will be "Separate but Equal, The Law Must Be Enforced." Once again, at Duke University, I must again complete a rigid course of study as well as achieving a 3.8 grade point average. Along with the publication of my memoir "Biloxi Rhapsody," this may satisfy most of the requirements for a doctorate. There may be other strict parameters which must be met but this is the most stringent requirement. A mock synopsis of a dissertation, "Separate but Equal, The Law Must Be Enforced," is made available for review in this memoir. This is a mock synopsis (brief, narrative, or treatise) of a dissertation.

Dissertation
"Mock Synopsis of a Dissertation"

King James Bible "The Good News"

Edgar Allan Poe "The Raven"

Barbara Miller Sonnier my only Proofreader and Editor

"Separate but Equal, The Law Must Be Enforced"
"Mock Synopsis of a Dissertation"
(It is the law.)

By: Ronnie James Sonnier Louviere`
(Rhone` James Saunier Louviere`)

A Dissertation Presented to the
Faculty of Duke Graduate School
"Mock Synopsis of a Dissertation"

In Partial Fulfillment of the requirements for the Degree:

Doctor of Political Science/ Public Policy

(Sociology)

Acknowledgements

Barbara Miller, my Proofreader and Editor - who means more to me than she can ever imagine,

and

Barbara Miller Sonnier my wife who has helped to guide me from darkness to light.

and

Abilene Christian University my alma mater

"Separate but Equal, The Law Must Be Enforced"
"Mock Synopsis of a Dissertation")
 The law must be enforced at all public institutions, it is the law.

See: The US Supreme Court

"Plessy vs Ferguson"

and

"Brown vs Board of Education"

Historical Relevance:

Abraham Lincoln defines black slavery as their "Peculiar Condition."

"The War Between The States" was only in small part about slavery of blacks.

"Roots" The Kunta Kinte myth by Alex Haley is a fabrication of Haley's roots.

Mock Synopsis of a Dissertation:
"Separate but Equal, The Law Must Be Enforced"

Chapter One

Premise:
This is a formal discourse supporting the enforcement of forced integration utilizing and exploiting **Affirmative Action, through quotas to achieve racial minority islands, in public colleges and universities supported by taxes as required by federal mandate. Affirmative Action forces an unconstitutional, Fourteenth Amendment, with financial mandates and or burdens on states. The United States Supreme Court discerned and ruled on our Fourteenth Amendment.

Just as segregation was sanctioned in its time by the Federal Government, so must forced desegregation (integration) through Affirmative Action have its time limited. The single purpose of Affirmative Action is that of obtaining diversity with often non-citizens, using illegal aliens (when citizens will not consent to being recruited) of color in order to achieve measured inclusion (approved statistical quotas) for racial equality in public institutions of higher learning.

Forced desegregation (integration based on statistical quotas forced specifically on individual states which have the inherent right to stand in opposition) must not end now that blacks are no longer the predominant minority (a shift in culture not withstanding). Most specifically the failure of historically all black colleges to statistically prove diversity (recruitment of sufficient whites to meet federally required quotas) in part as achievement when compared to historically all white (and other, but not people of color) public institutions such as The University of Mississippi, The University of Southern Mississippi, and The University of Alabama should be addressed.

Mock Synopsis of a Dissertation:
"Separate but Equal, The Law Must Be Enforced"

Chapter Two

Increasing demands and diminishing returns on this Unique Republic's (The United States of America) investments must be weighed and compared to historical facts which measure and account for the undeniable decline in learning and or a failure to achieve Self Reliance by the black race (they have imposed a form of enslavement of their mind on themselves), thereby sanctioning within their institutions no testing, only perhaps hard work, and a showing in their eyes to their professors that learning (osmosis education) has been adequately accomplished (a perpetuated myth).

Separate but equal must not apply, must not be legal, to the separation of historically all black institutions of learning from all other races and or cultures, whereas, all other races are excluded from receiving similar or equal privileges (not state or federal rights) as measured and dispensed by state and federal formulas (quota systems), thereby sanctioning de facto segregation at all education institutions separate and distinct from Historically All Black Colleges (such as five in Columbia, South Carolina and or public K12 schools as in certain districts in Little Rock, Arkansas).

Forced segregation is no longer governed equally by implementation of legislation or law. The white race has become the minority and is now the beneficiary of the living intent of the law. The law must be enforced regardless of which race (DNA curve proven) or culture is now the recipient or beneficiary, so to speak, as the new "Raisin in the Sun."

Note: "Raisin in the Sun," a play by Lorraine Hansberry (1959), and also a poem (which first appeared in 1951) by Langston Hughes called "Harlem" or "A Dream

Deferred," is about a black person's moral rights to a home. The lead character of the movie, play or poem is black and has certain moral rights to a home which he obtains in the suburbs of South Chicago, Illinois.

"Harlem"

By: Langston Hughes (published, 1951)

What happens to a dream deferred?
Does it dry up
like a raisin in the sun?
Or fester like a sore
And then run?
Does it stink like rotten meat?
Or crust and sugar over
like a syrupy sweet?
Maybe it just sags
like a heavy load.
Or does it explode?

Mock Synopsis of a Dissertation:
"Separate but Equal, The Law Must Be Enforced"

Chapter Three

To the contrary, the moral issue no longer stands the test of morality, time, and or dispensation of public funds, whereas blacks (not all are verifiable African American Citizens, case in point, Barrack Hussein Obama eventually felt he had to prove his birth in Hawaii to an American citizen mother and Kenyan father) disproportionately have failed the same tests (morality, time and financial dispensation) to succeed with equal treatment while funds, tax payer dollars, have been disproportionately distributed to achieve racial equality and not mental learning parity. Black (African American Citizens) institutions unto themselves have failed the test they imposed on others, especially those of European descent (Caucasoid, Europid, or Europoid).

Blacks have become unequal in that they have set themselves apart as a separate state within The Republic, and are therefore, a State (Black African Island) or Nation (Black African Archipelago) unto themselves. Ayers, (Caucasoid), King and Obama (both Black) embraced Black Liberation Theology (taught at Reverend Jeremiah Wright's church in Chicago, Illinois) not qualifying as citizens for separate unequal (more than equal), Separate but Equal in the spirit of more fair jurisprudence. Jurisprudence for themselves to be taken from dispensation and enumerations of taxes paid by all other races (cultures such as Caucasoid, Europid, or Europoid) of this Republic (The United States of America, 50 separate, but equal states).

The worm has turned and other than blacks have necessarily qualified for the fruits intended for them. The law is not forgiving and must be enforced without regard to past enslavement when the law favored one race over another based on necessary bias and challenge for other ethnicities to achieve equality for blacks. The Law Must Be Enforced.

Mock Synopsis of a Dissertation:
"Separate but Equal, The Law Must Be Enforced"

Chapter Four

It is not a requirement that someone, anyone, must pay taxes to become a citizen. As a citizen one must pay their predetermined tax amount in accordance with a schedule approved by Congress and The President of The United States of America to be collected by the Internal Revenue Service (IRS).

All black public education institutions have historically claimed tax exemptions and (claiming federal and state grants, subsidies, and financing) under the auspices of undefined, but declared forgiveness with appeasement and or reparations for black slavery or "their peculiar condition" as delicately defined by Abraham Lincoln.

My argument is concisely put that if you, any race, are systematically excluded from access to any college campus for any reason (failure to meet federally mandated quotas) Separate but Equal if being enforced by that institutions administration and the institution is in violation of The United States Constitution and applicable amendments and civil statutes, both State and Federal.

Minority enrollment in higher education has been on the rise, according to a 2010 Pew Research Center study, with Hispanic enrollment increasing the fastest. Pew found that whites made up sixty-two percent of the freshman class at four-year institutions in 2008, down from eighty-three percent in 1976. (That is about the same as the percentage of whites in the larger population, although the percentage of minorities among young people is higher.)

Mock Synopsis of a Dissertation:
"Separate but Equal, The Law Must Be Enforced"

Chapter Five

Nevertheless, the percentages of Black and Hispanic young people enrolled in higher education are still lower than those of Whites and Asians. Affirmative Action in college admissions was on the Supreme Court docket again in 2012 (but moved out to 2013) after a white student, Abigail Fisher, challenged a University of Texas (Austin, Texas) program meant to promote diversity on The University of Texas campuses.

In the 2003 University of Michigan case, Grutter v. Bollinger, although Justice Kennedy sided with the conservatives who wanted to strike down the school's use of race in admissions, Kennedy wrote a separate opinion, distancing himself from their more hard line views. Justice Kennedy wrote, "A racial quota can be the most divisive of all policies, containing within it the potential to destroy confidence in The Constitution and in the idea of equality, yet race might play a role as a modest factor among many others."

The University of Texas officials insist and the lower courts have agreed, that race was just one factor among many that was used to admit a small pool of students (under ten percent). We will see if their program is one of the instances of schools using race in admissions that Justice Kennedy deems permissible.

Mock Synopsis of a Dissertation:
"Separate but Equal, The Law Must Be Enforced"

Chapter Six

The United States Supreme Court will determine if being white is sufficient cause for Ms. Abigail Fisher, (a University of Texas student at the time) to claim discrimination and her placement in a University of Texas education department (her white race a factor verifiable with an authentic American birth certificate).

Additional comments regarding Affirmative Action:

**Affirmative Action legislation was approved in 1960 by Richard Milhous Nixon, President of The United States of America. The legislation as passed was well intended but grew into a monster like an out of control plague, a regular Frankenstein, which continues to haunt our nation as it robs from one to give to another. Affirmative Action spread the wealth of jobs through the egregious act of reverse discrimination to try and right a wrong which had been improperly invented for the appeasement of one minority while disturbing forever the proper assimilation of the total American culture.

This approved legislation has no boundaries as it has become self-evident. Affirmative Action is now an action which is not affirmative at all, and has far reaching tentacles spreading as a mental plague. This plague has no medicinal cure as it continues to devastate our Republic with an ever worsening sin of reverse discrimination, pitting brother against brother, and sister against sister, repeating our Civil War, The War Between The States. The prolonged war between the blue and the gray has now re-emerged as the new war between the red and blue division in our election process, and reparations/appeasement is an old term with evil meaning.

Incident: "My Treasures"

My Princess:

Following Vietnam I was stationed in Bamberg, Germany, 3rd Division 15th Infantry and later the 4th Armored Division out of France. I lived on the army post from August through September of 1962. Barbara joined me in Germany in late September of 1962, and we lived a few blocks off post (on the economy). Mrs. Heinze was our landlady at 26 Adam Saenger Strasse. Our attic style apartment was on the third floor of her house.

About ten months later we moved to 69 Stauffenburger Strasse. We occupied a small garden house owned by a nice German family. We were surrounded by fruit trees and Rose gardens. (I remember that our landlady gave Barbara nineteen roses on her nineteenth birthday; each rose was a different long-stemmed variety of rose.) Our little house was a short walk to the main gate of the Army Post.

While we were living on Adam Saenger we discovered that Barbara was pregnant with our first child. We used an old wives trick of dangling a needle over Barbara's stomach to determine that we were, possibly, going to have a girl. Barbara chose her name before she was born, and we both decided that her name would be Scarlett Lynn Sonnier.

Barbara visited the local Army Dispensary for prenatal checkups and was told that when she went into labor she would be transported by helicopter to the Wurzburg Army Hospital fifty miles away for delivery.

Scarlett, being of French and Irish heritage, would prove to be a regular firebrand and just as beautiful as Scarlett O'Hara. Our Scarlett's namesake is the heroine of

Margaret Mitchell's book, "Gone with the Wind." (Vivien Leigh played Scarlett O'Hara in the movie version of the book.)

The time came for us to go to Wurzburg for delivery, but the helicopter was already being used by other expectant parents. We were told that we would go by Army Ambulance and that they would stop by our apartment for Barbara to grab a bag.

Our nurse was a Lieutenant Colonel, seasoned, harsh, and abrupt, with an abundance of gold hash marks on both her sleeves. The Lt. Col. had a no nonsense air and she calmly took charge of Barbara's care. She put Barbara's mind at ease with the assurance that if necessary, she would deliver the baby in the ambulance. The nurse told us that she had delivered numerous babies and would try her best to get us to the Wurzburg Army Hospital before delivery became necessary.

The nurse placed Barbara in the front of the ambulance next to the driver, and she and I got in the back of the vehicle. She told the driver that he was to proceed with care, no bumpy ride. We headed for the main gate, at this point we were stopped and the driver was ordered by the guards to get out of the vehicle and show the papers authorizing our departure. The discussion went on for a couple of minutes.

Our nurse, Lt. Col., moved forward between the seats and stuck her head out and gave orders to get the hell out of her way. The Lt. Col. said, "My baby will not be born in this vehicle at the main gate." With recognition of the Lt. Col., the guards at the gate snapped to attention and said, "Yes Mam, please pass." Apparently they knew that she meant business.

Our nurse told us that she had been at The Normandy Beach Invasion and had driven a jeep for Lt. Colonel Benjamin Verdervoort (John Wayne's character in "The

Longest Day"). She also told us that she had consulted on the movie set of "The Longest Day." As this wonderful woman hero told us her story, I was very confident in her and could see the look of relaxation and confidence Barbara had in her. We knew our family was in the best possible hands.

When we arrived at the US Army Wurzburg Post Hospital in Wurzburg, Germany, waves of helpful medical personnel descended on our ambulance rendering immediate assistance. All the military personnel knew the history of our nurse at Normandy Beach and other World War II information about her. My family to be had experienced a very special gift of professionalism and dedication to duty from a US Army Nurse, Our Angel.

Marge and Gene Knoploh, Gene was one of my Army mates, were a little older than us and more mature. We had our first children, both girls, very close together. Barbara and I appreciated their friendship, then and now. We have exchanged season's greetings for years, and managed to visit once. We love them and cherish their friendship. Gene and Marge are "Giant Oak Trees Adorned With Spanish Moss."

Scarlett was born on July 3, 1963. Scarlett completed her BA Degree and excels in her chosen profession of IT Management. We love you very much Princess. Assimilation.

Poem "Untitled"

By: Scarlett Lynn Sonnier, written when an adolescent, undated

With ruins laying all around,
and weeds that cover all the ground.

For life has been gone for long,
with no one singing their favorite song.

219

And birds don't even stop their flite,
for such an ugly pitiful site.

And the people stare and ask "Why?"
such a beautiful town had to die.

My Prince:
My wonderful dream comes true. My, our first born son,
My Prince was born on February 10, 1965. While
Scarlett was My Princess and lights up my life, it was
Bryan Keith Sonnier who solidified it. Bryan had the
biggest most beautiful blue eyes, a window into his soul, a
good beautiful soul, truly a gift from God.

Bryan was never subservient or humble in spirit, but was
gifted to have humility. Bryan's humility inspired him to
help anyone at any time. He cared for those less fortunate
than himself and it was very apparent that anyone that met
Bryan grew to love him.

Bryan was the epitome of "tall, dark and handsome." He
stood six feet two inches in height, large athletic frame,
dark hair, light blue eyes and an olive complexion.
Although gifted with God given humility, Bryan had a
temper, but he was comfortable in his own skin. Bryan
was a very rough and competent star football player in
high school and college.

Bryan served in the US Army for ten years, and his
chosen profession (which he excelled at) was IT
Management, computer technology at a large retirement
campus. Bryan had completed his Associates Degree
while living in Arizona, was near completion of his BS,
and was making plans for working on his Master's
Degree. Assimilation.

On a fateful day in late July 2008, Bryan as Coach of his
work softball team decided to play short stop (his regular
player was not available). At age forty-three, a Perfect
Storm of humidity, exertion, added to his enlarged heart

took his life. (The coroner told us that Bryan was in perfect health, although his heart was enlarged, there was nothing wrong with it. Bryan's heart was not damaged due to a heart attack. Bryan had been dieting and had not been taking in the proper nutrients to sustain his body, he literally ran out of electricity to run his heart.)

Barbara and I were and still are devastated. Our son's laugh was infectious and at the end of our periodic telephone conversations (we either called him or he called us every couple of weeks) he would lower his voice and drag out "I love you."

The only reason that Barbara and I still remain sane, after Bryan's sudden loss, is that as Bible studying Christians, we know that Bryan is in Paradise with God Our Heavenly Father (date of arrival July 25, 2008). Bryan is a "Giant Oak Tree Adorned With Spanish Moss." We love you Son, and miss you every minute of every day. Assimilation.

My Artist (and Dillon):
It is most difficult to relate the circumstances of my son Sean Christopher Sonnier, born May 3, 1966, without including his attachment to Dillon our little red Golden Retriever.

This account is of a time after Christopher (Chris) had completed college art courses at a junior college in Freeport, Illinois, and taken courses at three other junior colleges. Chris is and has always been an extraordinary artist. Chris joined the US Army a year out of high school, completed training and was stationed at Fort Ord, California with The Nights of The Ninja. Chris' outfit was 7th Infantry, but they were sent on special assignment to Panama, pre Noriega ouster. Chris was assigned as a helicopter gunner and during maneuvers suffered traumas which led to Post Traumatic Stress Disorder, thus having his entire life affected by that assignment to Panama.

221

After completing his military obligation, and after discovering that he had physical, mental, and emotional problems, he stayed near us for many years. Barbara and I tried to help direct Chris and his finances so that he could enjoy as much of a normal life as possible. Due to Chris' illness he fights all help. In spite of himself, he continues to get treatment from Veterans Hospitals, and we encourage him to live independently from us.

Necessarily this reflection on Chris brings to note his/our Angel, Dillon. One cold afternoon I was grilling behind our house on a ridge in Woodlawn, Virginia. Barbara came to the back door and said, "When the black and white dog comes up here from the wood line run him off."

A short time later Barbara came to the door again and asked, "Have you seen that black and white dog?" I told her, "Yes, I ran it off." I continued to relate to her, "I also saw a reddish dog, tried to run him off, but he is over there. When I tried once more to get him to leave, he cowered and crawled toward me wagging his tail." We both noted that he was emaciated and looked like he had been mistreated.

Barbara and I both started talking quietly and encouragingly to the red dog. The dog approached us, came up to us and let Barbara put her hand under his nose. Barbara said, "This is a nice dog, we need to feed him and provide a pallet outside our back step for him." I agreed, it was going to be in the 20's that night.

(I thought that the dog had probably been caged to be used in dog fights. Michael V's dog fighting encampment was over thirty miles north of our home, but these dog fighting rings obtained dogs from different areas.)

We had no dog food, but Barbara made him several slices of warm buttered toast topped with cinnamon sugar and cane syrup (she put the food which she had cut into bite-sized pieces on a paper plate). Barbara brought the plate of food and cautiously sat it down, and we encouraged the dog to eat. While the dog ate Barbara talked to him and he allowed her to pat him on the back while he was he eating. She also put her hand toward his food, and he did not growl (this is a sign of a very good dog).

After we went inside we discussed keeping the dog if he was still around the next morning. We figured the puppy was about six months old. The puppy was so thin that his ribs could be seen and his skin was dry and scaly. He was at our back step the next morning. Barbara fed him and gave him fresh water. We decided to name him Dillon after Marshall Matt Dillon of Gunsmoke fame (we were currently watching reruns of Gunsmoke starring James Arness).

We went to Wal-Mart and purchased food, dish, etc., and made Dillon a bed in a large television box we had in our garage. In the pet department at Wal-Mart Barbara found pet clothes (wipes) to use to clean Dillon. She wiped and brushed him twice a day until his red hair was beautiful and the dryness left his skin. He started to fill out quickly.

We would bring Dillon in the house with us at night and he would not lie down; he paced continuously. We left him alone, and one night I was lying on our loveseat watching television with my left arm down encouraging Dillon to be petted. Dillon came over, I petted him and talked to him, he lay down and next thing we knew he was fast asleep on my arm. Seeing Dillon still and trusting and remembering how he was when he came to us, caused us both to cry. We enjoyed having Dillon as a new family member. Our home was located on a ridge with seven acres of woods surrounding it. Dillon learned to enjoy the outdoor space and became healthy. His coat became so red and beautiful that people took notice of him. He had a very loving personality, soul.

We had introduced Dillon to Chris while visiting him at the Salem Medical Center; they became buds very fast. Chris would visit us at our house in Woodlawn and it was evident that he and Dillon were developing a special friendship. We unselfishly allowed Dillon to go live with Chris in his townhouse in Salem, Virginia.

While Dillon had no formal therapy training, he had the heart and love for Chris to try and help Chris. When Chris would have a nightmare, Dillon would crawl close to Chris, and comfort him. We feel that Dillon absorbed a great deal of Chris' anguish and pain. We feel that Dillon slowly took on some of Chris' illness, helped Chris to carry his load. Dillon started having seizures after a few months with Chris, and after several years they were the cause of a stroke and our having to put him to sleep. We still love and miss Dillon terribly. During the ensuing years, Dillon was our dog and Chris' dog. We always allowed Dillon to choose if he wanted to stay home with Chris or go with us to his other home, or vice versa.

Unfortunately the US Army and Veterans Affairs do not recognize Post Traumatic Stress and accompanying mental disorders for full disability pay. Chris does not receive adequate money from combined VA Benefits and Social Security Disability Benefits, but he makes out. His illness makes it difficult for him to work; people in work places can be cruel. Chris receives adequate, but not superior help from the VA.

Chris (and Dillon) will always be two of our "Giant Oak Trees Adorned With Spanish Moss." We love you very much Chris, our Artist. We love you Dillon. Assimilated.

My Warrior:
My youngest son, Darren Ashley Sonnier was born on December 1, 1968. Our family always teased Darren about being the youngest in the family and having no seniority. Darren is extremely intelligent possessing a

very high IQ. Darren like his brothers loved to play football and received a football scholarship to college like his brother Bryan.

After attending Aurora University in Aurora, Illinois for a year, Darren decided to join the Army. Darren has traveled the world, served his country, retired from the military, and continues to assimilate.

When Darren was a youngster, he would make drawings of warrior soldiers with tattoos, wearing full military garb, bearing rifles, guns and knives. Darren always indicated he wanted to be a US Military warrior, and he made it happen as over the years with perseverance and dedication he built himself into a real dynamic individual. Darren once told us that he could do anything he set his mind to, and that is true. Darren is one of our elite, and he is not simply brawn, but has used his intellectual prowess to get a good college education.

Suffice it to say, Darren is a wonderful representative of the assimilation our Sonnier and Louviere` families have made into mainstream America. We love Darren very much, wish him well in his chosen life's works, and recognize he is another of our "Giant Oak Trees Adorned With Spanish Moss." Darren, your Mom and I love you very much. Assimilated.

"Shelter of a Song"

A Poem By: Rhone` Sonnier Louviere` completed, November, 2012

Moss hangs from my oak tree,
Just as lightning shooting down from cumulus clouds,
And leaves fall in the autumn,
Just as rain from the heavens onto this earth,
The replenishing of the moss begins anew,

Just as acorns flourish from the dew,
As my tree grows its branches long and strong,
It resembles good men who do no wrong,
As they seek to shelter us with God's Song.

Incident: "Dysfunctional Family"

Barbara my soulmate and I had already experienced some tumult in our young lives and God must have wanted us to witness certain incidences. Barbara is of English, Irish, French, some Choctaw descent, and I am of Cajun French descent. This is one heck of a gene pool and not because of cultural influences.

Our mothers had it tough, and our fathers had no clue as to how they could spare them the grief they were sufferring as ill equipped women in their unique circumstances (peculiar conditions).

Unfortunately for Barbara, I pursued her and threw her off her career path. She always planned to go to college, graduate, perhaps have a career, possibly someday marry a successful organized husband, and eventually have a loving family.

God was looking out for me, but I am afraid not as much for Barbara, whereas I contend that it was I who received the best of our marriage and years of family life together. I often wonder if perhaps God, in his infinite wisdom, joined Barbara Ann Miller and me together as man and wife as part of his plan.

In moving quite often because of my different jobs, for whatever reasons, we and our children experienced a very diverse cultural life and education. Our children were/are unafraid and bold. We always encouraged them and told them that they could do anything they set their minds and hearts to (in essence, You Do Need That). All four of our children matured with self-confidence and assurance in their abilities.

Each of our children attended college, worked and or joined the military and had some success. We believe each of our children chose their own life paths and experienced happiness and or unhappiness due to their

227

right to choose and their own intellects. Parents must allow their children to succeed or fail.

Barbara and I were the last to hear and or be told, by our daughter Scarlett, that we had a dysfunctional family (maybe we had pie in the sky expectations of rearing a close knit family that we would be able to enjoy our entire lives). Barbara and I were strict parents expecting the best from our children, but we did not realize that we were/are the culprits causing a dysfunctional cataclysm. True, we never promoted the Be Free Mentality of our daughter Scarlett's generation, The X Generation, a totally lost generation.

Scarlett was and is correct, we are a dysfunctional family (I first heard of our peculiar condition from her mouth). Years after this revelation and after a family squabble in exchanging e-mails (of all things), I wrote her a blood curdling e-mail and letter, which was accurate and unfortunately challenging but not wise, and I regretted it the moment I sent them. Sometimes the truth is better unspoken.

What is a dysfunctional family, a family fighting?" I recently asked my ninety-two year old father. Daddy replied while laughing out loud, "That is a feud, *querelle de famille.*" He then asked, "You have that too?" Daddy laughed again. I do not find our family feud funny, but Daddy seemed to feel that it was hilarious.

Daddy stopped laughing and said, "Tomorrow will stop all of that, yes." *"Demain s`arrête tout cela, oui."* I thought, life evolves and situations change and God gave us all free will to do as we please. Forrest Gump (from the movie starring Tom Hanks, Hanks won an Oscar for his performance) said, "Mama said life is like a box of chocolates, you never know what you are going to get."

Note: "Forrest Gump" is a 1994 American epic comedy-drama-romance film based on the 1986 novel of the same name by Winston Groom. While Forrest Gump was not intelligent, he was present at many historic moments in time. Throughout the book and movie his true love, Jenny eludes him. On July 6, 1994 Forest Gump while discussing his level of intelligence said, "Stupid is as stupid does." "Forrest Gump," the movie was directed by Robert Zemeckis.

At one point in time when Barbara and I felt that Scarlett was being quite disrespectful, Barbara said, "You need to show us (your parents) some respect." Scarlett responded to her Mother, "Then you need to show some to me."

Scarlett changed greatly once she left home to attend college and began to listen to the liberal agendas of her professors. She began to associate with people that were raised quite differently from her. A few years ago, Barbara and I were having a discussion with our son Chris regarding our fragmented family. Chris said, "We were raised in a good home, a home with values, then we went out into the world and interacted with people that were not raised in homes with two parents or in homes where values were enforced." Chris had made a very prophetic and intelligent well thought out observation. Assimilation is both functional and dysfunctional.

In the end, God will judge Barbara and I and our children; we did our best, we were not presented a blueprint on how to raise a perfect family. This I know, there must be more than this, something somewhere, somehow better than this.

Book of Micah, Chapter 7, Verse 6, King James Version of The Holy Bible *For the son dishonoureth the father, the daughter riseth up against her mother, the daughter-in-law against her mother-in-law; a man's enemies are the men in his own house.*

Book of Deuteronomy, Chapter 4, Verse 16, King James Version of The Holy Bible *Honour thy father and thy mother, as the Lord thy God hath commanded thee; that thy days may be prolonged and that it may go well with thee, in the land which the Lord thy God giveth thee.*

My Promise to my Children

I am your Parent. I will stalk you, flip out on you, drive you insane, be your worst nightmare and hunt you down like a bloodhound when needed because I love you! When you understand that, you will know you are a responsible adult. You will never find someone who loves, prays, cares and worries about you more than I do!

By: Unknown Author (original writing uses Mother not Parent)

Incident: "Teacher/Professor/Master"

"The love of learning, the sequestered nooks,
And all the sweet serenity of books."

By: Henry Wadsworth Longfellow, 1807 - 1882

Not everyone can write, not everyone can teach, they both take practice and experience to do well. On the occasions when the regular teacher is not available a Guest Teacher is necessarily selected from a pre-approved pool of Substitute Teachers, and this is where and when the first of many problems with student learning begins. There is no such thing as a viable substitute or alternative for the student's regular teacher or their parents.

I know this because I have been part of this transition and it begins with students asking at the door to the class-room, "Are you the Sub?" It is therefore my qualified educated opinion that there exists a more politically correct and acceptable alternative for a person accepting responsibility for a time in place of the parent.

I do not like the term Substitute or Sub, and the students do not like it either. It is demeaning to both the guest or visiting teacher and the students. Guest is the proper term to use. Guest Teacher is a more useable and digestible term and description than that of Substitute Teacher. The word Substitute has an unacceptable meaning and connotations in diverse languages and societies. The choice of names must be necessarily relegated to the decision of the most local individual school districts and each state, not the federal education system and most certainly not the Federal Department of Education. Pro-viding substitute is acceptable, so be it.

When you consider a person to be a guest in your home or business you welcome them wholeheartedly with respect while preserving your own dignity and theirs as well. Names and titles do matter to children. My home is your

231

home. *Ma maison est votre maison.* This is a proper and respectful welcome and even implies the security of your guest is your concern and your friendship a given.

Substitute (you are or you are not the teacher) is not a designation assuring complete acceptance of this awesome responsibility, in place of the parent. *A la place de la mere.* When I accept a teaching assignment, I consider myself a guest at the school, and as such must as best I can follow the teacher's plans and curriculum left for my use that day.

When there is no plan and or activity it becomes my responsibility to provide an opportunity for learning which will require their attention and best behavior. I usually accomplish getting and keeping students attention with stories, whereas I am a storyteller extraordinaire.

I am the most disheartened when I am in a class room and administration announces a moment of silence and students do not honor this, they keep playing and making noise. After a moment of silence the office administrator says please stand for The Pledge of Allegiance (or, vice versa). Many of the students do not stand or recite The Pledge, the students continue to play and make noise. Disrespect is rampant. It is against the Law for a teacher to lead the students in prayer or The Pledge of Allegiance. I contend that this display of nonchalance is a major sign of moral decay.

As my teaching days appear to be numbered, and perhaps soon to come to an end, I imagine again that I feel the earth vibrate and purr as my whistling and tooting train approaches me, and I consider getting aboard for yet another journey away from guest teaching.

I love trains and *sojournes* of the mind. This book is that journey of my mind in which I reflect on some of the best of my own stories which I have presented in classes, but never put to pen or paper. It is true "Biloxi Rhapsody" is a collection of storytelling of incidents and poetry describing the assimilation of my family into the American culture, and is my best account of our Survival of the Fittest. Fact is, "Biloxi Rhapsody" is much more than stories it is my soulmate, my Barbara, she is my Biloxi Rhapsody.

Some of my mental sojourns are like a freight train running through my head (excerpt of lyrics from a Bruce Springsteen song). I love storytelling and my personal favorite from "Biloxi Rhapsody" is The Alligator That Barked where a little girl named Lois taught me about alligators. Lois caused me to realize my limitations. I found out that I could not run as fast as I thought I could, and this realization caused me to imagine myself as Boy, Son of Tarzan, rather than Hop-A-Long Cassidy (actor William Boyd) who was not a good runner but a good rider.

Every incident I wrote about explains assimilation and foreshadows future incidents where I utilize that which I have learned from my mentors. Storytelling is educational and inspirational. The Alligator that Barked foreshadowed the most brutal incident of my life. That incident was when I lay hurt under the bodies of my Brothers in a large warehouse in Vietnam, knowing and hearing crocodiles were prowling ever closer. In Three Survived, I had first been called "Pop."

Students call me Pop and often ask me, "Are you Pop, The Storyteller?" I respond with, "That's me, yes, I am that Pop."

Incident: "Evangeline II"

Evangeline, the epic poem by Henry Wadsworth Longfellow, is not factual about anyone French human being named Evangeline or another French human being named Gabriel. "Evangeline," the poem, as written by Longfellow is quite simply not true (again, while historical facts are verifiable and true, the main characters Evangeline and Gabriel were not and are not real people, though perhaps they are representative of a type of people, the Cajuns of the Gulf Coast Regions of the United States).

"Biloxi Rhapsody" is not completely factual dialog or a true depiction of all characters or incidents. While this account of Louviere` and or Sonnier everyday life is not precise dialog, it is truly Cajun assimilation into American culture particularly in Louisiana, Mississippi, and Texas. Acadiana in Louisiana is comprised of about twenty-two parishes. It forms a triangle inclusive of Lake Charles at the west to Grand Isle at the east with Pointe Coupee at the apex.

From 1765 to 1785, the Acadians were the largest nationality to settle in this area. Acadian culture was the most dominant culture in many places, although other diverse nationalities were evident. Many diverse cultures were added to the Acadians which assimilated into a variation of the Acadian culture now known as Cajun (Caucasian Children of Israel).

Book of Jeremiah, Chapter 4, Verses 11 & 12, New King James Version of The Holy Bible *At that time it will be said to this people and to Jerusalem, a dry wind of the desolate heights blows in the wilderness toward the daughter of My People not to fan or to cleanse; A wind too strong for these will come for Me; Now I will also speak judgment against them.*

"At home the pendulum seems to swing away from the promise of real change: the change from little boys and little girls picking cotton to children reading and writing and wearing shoes and eating every day and one day getting to vote or getting to influence their father's or their brother's vote. It's like being pregnant. You are or you are not. A child has those things or does not." An Excerpt From: "The Wind Done Gone," by Alice Randall.

I, Rhone` Sonnier Louviere`, long for the mornings in the kitchen with my Mama and the aroma emanating from her black iron skillet as she cooked pork sausage and eggs side by side. The eggs cooked in the sausage fat making a heavenly blend. I remember that the combination of scents permeated our home and floated through our windows out into the neighborhood, tantalizing the senses of our neighbors. I had the feeling that everyone for miles around envied me and my place in Mama's kitchen.

I have spent my entire life experiencing and keeping my thoughts locked away in a book in my mind. This, My Memoir, was begging for escape onto pages others could put their hands on, read and possibly comprehend, and I hope appreciate. The inner recesses of my mind have been spilled onto these pages, and now I am as vulnerable as Hop-a-Long Cassidy, Boy and Bomba, long gone.

I am beyond middle age and I have put the past in letters forming English and French words. This I have done as I remember each event (incident), thereby creating a memoir which will have meaning only each reader can judge as worthy and credible through, I trust, each their own wisdom and gift of discernment.

My father (Daddy), Dalton Sonnier, is ninety-two years of age and lives in Ocean Springs, Mississippi. My Father has forgotten, as have I, most of his Acadian Cajun French language (his fault and mine), but he speaks in a distinct French dialect, with a rich Cajun accent. I have no accent, I have been told this many times by many people.

Daddy is hard of hearing, as am I, which makes telephone communication difficult. When having long distance conversations, shouting back and forth, we either cannot hear one another or we cannot understand one another. Our conversations can be quite hilarious. Barbara reminds me to try and not disturb our neighbors. During many of these conversations with my Dad, I have researched about events (incidents) and family, revisiting our past with my Daddy is extremely emotional for both of us.

I have, as many other authors have done before, looked back and forward preparing to sort out and rearrange the compartments of my thoughts in my mind, shredding some while lifting up and offering all of my thoughts to my God for his blessings in this novel "Biloxi Rhapsody," (The Memoirs of a Storyteller).

Each night at the end of the day, I walk to the foot of the bed and say, "I guess I get to sleep with Barbara again." "Yes, you do!" Barbara Miller Sonnier, "Biloxi Rhapsody," answers, welcoming me to another night of dreams, perhaps to be shared another day.

"The Arrow and the Song"

By Henry Wadsworth Longfellow, 1807-1882

"I shot an arrow into the air,
It fell to earth, I knew not where;
For, so swiftly it flew, the sight
Could not follow it in its flight.

I breathed a song into the air,
It fell to earth, I knew not where;
For who has sight so keen and strong,
That it can follow the flight of song?

Long, long afterward, in an oak
I found the arrow, still unbroken;
And the song, from beginning to end,
I found again in the heart of a friend."

Biloxi Rhapsody Encore, my next book, is in my mind
waiting to be put in words.

finis (francais)
(Finished)

Postscript

In "The Alligator That Barked," Gumbo gave his life protecting Rhone` Sonnier Louviere` and Lois Hebert, and his heroism foreshadowed an event in "Three Survived."
Rhone` Sonnier Louviere`

Nation, May 30, 2002, updated 03:01 a.m. ET
"When they eat your dog, they're not so cute" by: Deborah Sharp, USA Today
"When they weigh 600 pounds and eat your dog for lunch, they're not so cute anymore," says Lt. Del Teagan, an alligator specialist with Florida's Fish and Wildlife Conservation Commission.

If attacked, raise a ruckus and a fight. "Resist as best you can," says Henry Cabbage, spokesman for Florida's wildlife commission. "Any predator favors prey it can easily overcome." Source: USA Today research.
ClarionLedger.com (A Gannett Company)

Most Alligators in Mississippi? Jackson, Hancock, Harrison counties ....
Written by: The Associated Press, 10:26 a.m., September 27, 2012

Gulfport - The lower three counties of South Mississippi are home to 38 percent of the state's alligators.
Ricky Flynt, alligator coordinator for the Mississippi Department of Wildlife, Fisheries and Parks –
"It's obvious that part of the country has traditionally been home to alligators since any records we have on file. The coastal area has always been part of their natural range."
"In fact, we have never had a reported alligator attack on humans in Mississippi. That's all good."

Acknowledgements:

Hop-a-Long Cassidy a fictional cowboy hero created in 1904 by Clarence E. Mulford.

Tarzan's son Boy and Bomba the Jungle Boy, created by Edgar Rice Burroughs.

"Louisiana," lyrics by Randy Newman," No infringement intended, used for educating only.

"The saltwater crocodile was historically found throughout Southeast Asia, but is now extinct throughout much of this range. It is probable that the only country in Indochina still harboring wild populations of this species is Myanmar, although saltwater crocodiles were once very common in the Mekong Delta (from where they disappeared in the 1980's) and other river systems.

Reference: "Crocodile kills man in wildlife sanctuary - World news - World environment - msnbc.com." MSNBC. 2009-04-20. Retrieved 2010-08-18.

"The saltwater crocodiles are the largest crocodilians in existence, in addition to being highly opportunistic and territorial predators when compared to other crocodilians (such as the American alligator and other smaller species of crocodiles and caimans). They have a strong tendency to treat humans in their territory as prey, and have a long history of attacking and consuming humans who stray into their territory. In distinct contrast to the American policy of encouraging a certain degree of habitat coexistence, the only safe policy for dealing with saltwater crocodiles is to avoid their territory whenever possible as they tend to be highly aggressive when encroached upon."

Reference: Guggisberg, C.A.W. (1972). Crocodiles: Their Natural History, Folklore, and Conservation.

Newton Abbot: David & Charles p. 195. ISBN 0-7153-5272-5.

Harper Lee's novel, "To Kill a Mocking Bird" inspired my writing about children and diversity.

Carl Bernstein and Bob Woodward's book, "All the President's Men" caused me to write about law and politics.

Barbara Miller Sonnier and our children Scarlett, Bryan, Sean (Chris), and Darren; Mervin Joseph Sonnier, brother; Judy Sonnier Domonousky, sister; Antony (Tony) Arakkal, Indian Angel, best mate; Rebecca Miller, best friend; Allen "Pete" Sonnier, lifelong friend; Tommy Hebert, cousin, Decorated Vietnam War Veteran; Sylvester Louviere`, grandfather; Laura Giotte Louviere`, grandmother; Cyrus Bruce (Bit) Louviere`, uncle; Ursin Sonnier, grandfather; Olivia Sonnier, grandmother; Mary Jane Waltman Hunne Goff. Grandma Hon, great-grandmother-in-law (Choctaw/Irish); Lois Hebert, childhood angel; Marvin and Judy Anglada, Hurricane Camille angels, Charlotte Webb Wise and Ray Wise, good neighbors; Leonard and Shirley McMurrian, friends and Biloxi Magnolia Lodge; Bobby Scarborough, friend and Biloxi Magnolia Lodge; Bob Garrison, mentor, Biloxi Indian's Basketball Coach; and all relatives: Miller, Goff, Waltman, Simmons, Louviere`, Sonnier, Hulin, Breau, Hebert, Seymour, Hill, Illich ....

EPILOGUE

(Reference back to page 215 of
Mock Synopsis of Dissertation)

SUPREME COURT OF THE UNITED STATES

No. 11-345

ABIGAIL NOEL FISHER, PETITIONER V. THE

UNIVERSITY OF TEXAS AT AUSTIN Et. al.

ON WRIT OF CERTIORARI TO THE United States

COURT OF APPEALS FOR THE FIFTH CIRCUIT

(June 24, 2013)

JUSTICE KENNEDY delivered the opinion of the Court.

"Because the Court of Appeals did not apply the correct standard of strict scrutiny in its decision affirming the District Court's grant of summary judgement to the University was incorrect; that decision is vacated; and the case is remanded for further proceedings."

Rhone' Sonnier Louviere'
February 10, 2014